CORE OF A MAN

THE BLUEPRINT TO BE AN AMAZING MAN

JOHN BELL

WESTBOW
PRESS®
A DIVISION OF THOMAS NELSON
& ZONDERVAN

WestBow Press books may be ordered through booksellers or by contacting:

WestBow Press
A Division of Thomas Nelson & Zondervan
1663 Liberty Drive
Bloomington, IN 47403
www.westbowpress.com
844-714-3454

All scripture quotations are taken from the World English Bible. Public domain.

ISBN: 978-1-9736-9933-0 (sc)
ISBN: 978-1-9736-9934-7 (hc)
ISBN: 978-1-9736-9932-3 (e)

Library of Congress Control Number: 2023909762

Print information available on the last page.

WestBow Press rev. date: 09/23/2023

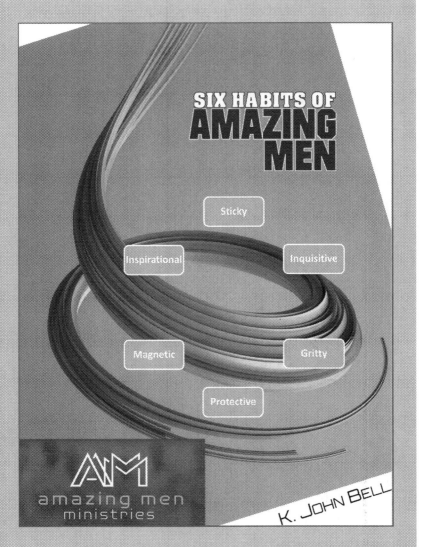

SIX HABITS OF
AMAZING
MEN

Sticky

Inspirational

Inquisitive

Magnetic

Gritty

Protective

AM
amazing men
ministries

K. JOHN BELL

Contents

Foreword

A sage once advised, "Learn from the mistakes of others; you can't possibly live long enough to make them all yourself." If you're like me, you've made many mistakes. But there's hope!

You have in your hands a book that I wish I had read fifty years ago. If I had, my life would have taken a much better trajectory and been more successful, healthy, and joyful. Packed into these pages is a wealth of extremely practical advice that comes from many sources, including ancient wisdom, leading-edge research, and a long life dedicated to helping others become the men they were designed to be.

The author, John Bell, speaks with authority on what it means to be an amazing man and how to become one. Over the years, as I have worked for him and have observed him, I have seen firsthand how he truly models the amazing life. John's relationship with me has modeled the process of deep friendships that this book describes. He and I have gone from being mere buddies to friends for life. I am truly fortunate that I know he will always be there for me—a man I can and do call on my best days and my worst days.

It is true that "Iron sharpens iron, and one man sharpens another." I believe that a corollary to this is "Marshmallows don't sharpen marshmallows." Men who want to grow cannot be afraid of a few sparks. It's part of the process. The honesty and vulnerability that John and I share in our relationship has enabled us both to grow and experience exciting synergies that keep us motivated. When we work together on a project, we often feel exhilarated by what we've been able to accomplish. You can build these kinds of friendships too.

To become an amazing man takes hard work, and it's never-ending. I agree with what John writes. "I'm still working at it." The good news, though, is that the "years that the locusts have eaten" can be restored. I know this firsthand.

I encourage each man who picks up this book to make a commitment to be all that he can be. With the help of other good men, and that of the Lord, you can revitalize your relationships and your life. With John, I challenge you to clarify your identity and to fulfill your dreams and your destiny, starting right here, right now.

Mark Dattoli
Friend and colleague

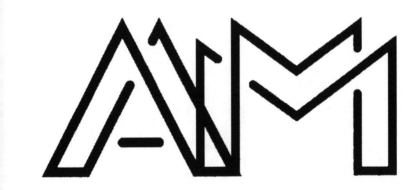

Introduction

Who Doesn't Want to Be Amazing?

When I was a little boy, I wanted to be a cowboy. Not any cowboy but one of the good guys. There was always a bully or a schemer in the saloon or the town who took advantage of everyone—the women, the card players, the bartenders, the other cowboys, and sometimes even the sheriff. Everyone was afraid; everyone was quiet. Then the good guy would show up. He wasn't afraid. He knew what was right and he knew how to protect others. He would stand up to the predator. Sometimes standing up to him was enough, but sometimes it wasn't. It didn't matter; the good guy would always do whatever was needed to remove the threat. I wanted to be that guy. He was amazing!

In 2015, I started a consulting, mentoring, and coaching group. My friend Tom Cole asked me what I was going to call it. I said, "Amazing Men." He said, "John, who doesn't want to be amazing?" Exactly.

Amazing men aren't born; they're formed through the crucible of life. Amazing men start off just like every other man.

Eugene O'Neill wrote, "Man is born broken. He lives by mending. The grace of God is glue."

Mending takes a long time, maybe a whole life. We will explore that in this book. As we work through our brokenness, we can become amazing.

What Is an Amazing Man?

First, here's what it's not: It's not a great jump shot or accumulating great fortune or fame. It's not being handsome or athletic or having a big brain. You can have all that and still be a jerk. I've met plenty of those guys and couldn't wait to get away.

When you look up the word *amazing*, here is what you find:

- "astonishing, astounding, stunning"
- and my favorite: "extraordinarily impressive"

Let's put that together. *An amazing man lives an amazing life that is extraordinarily impressive. He learns, loves, and leads in an amazing way.*

This is what makes him impressive. He is

- sticky
- inquisitive
- gritty
- protective
- magnetic
- inspirational

In this book, we'll explore each of these six dimensions.
You really can become amazing!
Let me give you a challenge as we begin.

> Join me, brothers, not in another men's event or movement but in the pursuit of our healing, honesty, and the joy of becoming the men God intended for us to be. Take the initiative; speak up; get off of the sidelines!
>
> Reject the voice of shame that wants you to shut up and hide. Come forth and be real, not with everyone but with a

few good men. This is our rebellion against the status quo, against our false selves, and against the male caricatures that others have drawn for us.

Let's step out of the herd and create a new way for men. Forging friendships with one another that stand the test of conflict and time, our friendships will make us better husbands, better fathers, and better men.

Let's journey together toward a better identity as we accept the challenge that this journey will be daunting. Let us commit to changing the world of men, one man at a time, starting with ourselves and our friends.

Introductory Questions

1. When you were a boy, what did you dream you would be as a man?

2. Where are you today as a man? As we age, we all have regrets and disappointments when we reflect upon our lives. What are yours?

3. Do you see yourself learning, loving, and leading in amazing ways?

4. Have you ever evaluated yourself in the six dimensions identified in this chapter: sticky, inquisitive, gritty, protective, magnetic, inspirational?

5. Are you ready to dig deep and begin to make changes that will help you be an amazing man?

6. Who will you enlist to support you on your journey to amazing manhood?

Chapter 1

HOW THIS BOOK CAN HELP

Why Is This Book Different?

This book

- blends ancient wisdom and modern science
- is aspirational
- targets men
- focuses on joy
- links joy to character change

❖ Ancient Wisdom and Modern Science

Wisdom means skill, shrewdness, expertise, or masterful understanding. Wisdom is often used in relation to the arts of war, governing, diplomacy, or discernment. Generally speaking, this wisdom is accessible to anyone. It doesn't come from miraculous visions but by careful observation of everyday life as well as deference to tradition. Wisdom enables an individual to manage his or her life and to achieve success against insurmountable odds. Wisdom is not neutral. Ancient wisdom is God centered, which makes God-pleasing wisdom inaccessible except by God's grace. Fearing God brings a certain kind of clarity to life—both moral and mental—and makes possible the use of godly insight and understanding. Ancient wisdom not only teaches us how to live but also teaches us how to die. It teaches us what it means to face the inevitability of death and to view it with the perspective of faith. Embracing this wisdom allows us to set our sights on eternity and on becoming amazing along the way.

Modern brain science supports ancient wisdom. Breakthroughs in neuroscience tell us how our brains function at an optimal level. Pioneering work has been done in the last few decades by doctors, such as Allan Schore, Jim Wilder, Timothy R. Jennings, Daniel A. Amen, Marian Diamond, and Caroline Leaf. For example, ancient wisdom stresses the importance of forgiveness, even though estrangement and revenge are often our automatic responses. However, biochemical research demonstrates that a toxic chemical flood is released into our brains when we think vengeful thoughts. Microphotographs show how the chemicals that are released burn tunnels into the branches of our nerve cells. Dr. Leaf calls these burned-out brain cells "emotional black holes." They are empty spaces in the brain produced by an angry and bitter heart. But when we choose to forgive, the brain is enabled to grow new nerve fibers that fill in the black holes. Old memories can be replaced. Ancient wisdom told us that, and modern science has confirmed it.

❖ Aspirational: The Blueprint

This book is for men who want to be their best. It is based on the way men were supposed to be. In a perfect world, we wouldn't need amazing men; we would only need men. The word *amazing* also means "causing great surprise or wonder." The kind of men that we are aiming at in this book, *Amazing Men*, will cause surprise and wonder only because most men are not even close to what they were supposed to be.

The phrase "supposed to be" assumes that there was a blueprint or a plan for humankind. How do you answer the following questions?

- Where did we come from? (Origin)
- Why are we here? (Meaning)
- How do we live while we're here? (Morality)
- What happens when we die? (Destiny)

If we are here by an accidental explosion or as the result of random mutations, then the answer is nowhere and nothing. But if there was a designer, what was the blueprint? Even further, was the blueprint distinct between a man and a woman?

This book makes the assumption that there is a "supposed to be" and that there are distinctions between a man and a woman, not just physically but to our very core.

❖ Targets Men

Women and men should read this book, but it targets *men's* hearts. Why?

One of my favorite illustrations gives the answer.

There was a man who had a little boy he loved very much. Every day after work, the man would come home and play with the little boy. He spent most evenings playing with the little boy.

One night while the man was at work, he realized that he had extra work to do for the evening and wouldn't be able to play with his little boy. But he wanted to give the boy something to keep him busy. Looking around his office, he saw a magazine with a large map of the world on the cover. He got an idea. He removed the map and then patiently tore it up into small pieces. Then he put all the pieces in his coat pocket.

When he got home, the little boy came running to him and was ready to play. The man explained that he had extra work to do and couldn't play just now, but he led the little boy into the dining room. Taking out the pieces of the map, he spread them on the table. He explained that it was a map of the world and that by the time the little boy could put it back together, his extra work would be finished and they could both play. Surely this would keep the child busy for hours, he thought.

About twenty minutes later, the boy said, "OK, it's finished. Can we play now?"

The man was surprised, saying, "That's impossible. Let's see."

Sure enough, there was the picture of the world, all put together, every piece in its place.

The man said, "That's amazing! How did you do that?" The boy said, "It was simple. On the back of the page was a picture of a man. I figured that if I could get the man right, I could get the world right."

When men are *restored,* the world around them falls into place.

❖ The Fuel for an Amazing Life Is Joy

One of the great discoveries of Dr. Allan Schore is the importance of joy for healthy brain development. Dr. Schore defines joy as being with "someone who is glad to be with me" or "being the sparkle in someone's eye." We've learned that our brains and our lives only run on one of two things: joy or fear.

Many men have never experienced relational joy. Instead of joy, they feel emptiness. Their tank is empty; they are running on fumes. Jackson Brown even wrote a song about this entitled "Running on Empty." A solitary man is a dangerous man. But the information and the habits that we will discuss will enable you to fill your tank so that your joy bucket will be full.

❖ Joy and Character Change

We have all felt the knot in our stomach, our face turning red, our shoulders stiffen, and sweat break out. What is that? That's your body telling you your true character. Your brain controls and tells your body how to respond. Dr. Bessel van der Kolk titled his well-researched book *The Body Keeps the Score.*

Our character is the set of deep-seated, automatic responses to our relational environment. It is our instantaneous behavior to what is happening to us in real time. You can try all kinds of little techniques on your own: count to ten, take a time-out, or bite your tongue. But when you experience a negative emotion like anger, fear, sadness, disgust, shame, or despair, your true character comes out. That is what we need to change.

The only real antidote is a rhythm of joy and quiet. A reservoir of joy and the ability to quiet your heart will produce character change. Learning to make a *joy cocktail* will dilute the negative emotion. You will learn how to manage anger while maintaining your joy. That skill means you can always be your best self and live out of a new heart, even when negative emotions threaten to overwhelm you.

In the next chapter, we'll begin to look at the obstacles that stop most men from becoming amazing. Some are in plain sight; others are not. Overcoming them isn't easy, but it is worth it. Let's get started.

Questions for Chapter 1

1. This chapter says, "Ancient wisdom not only teaches us how to live but also teaches us how to die. It teaches us what it means to face the inevitability of death in faith. We set our sights on eternity and on becoming amazing." Have you ever come to a point in your life where you have resolved these questions about eternity for yourself? If not, why not interrupt your study of this book and do that soon?

2. Are there people in your life that you hold a grudge against? What would it take to settle this issue and release its grip on your life and health?

3. Do you agree that there is a blueprint for a man to aspire to?

4. How might your world "fall into place" if you, and the men around you, were restored to what is supposed to be?

5. Do you agree that "a solitary man is a dangerous man?" Solitary men are common. Are you one? Do you see any evidence of danger in your life?

6. Do you currently have a reservoir of relational joy in your life, a "rhythm of joy and quiet?" Can you list a handful of people who are glad when you show up?

7. Can you envision how a *joy cocktail* could help you make the character changes you would need to become a truly amazing man?

Chapter 2

THE OBSTACLE COURSE

Part 1
The Past

Whenever I take on a challenge, I like to know what I'm up against. Many of the obstacles to being amazing are in the future. I need a new way of thinking, a new way of practicing, and a new set of habits. We will get to those.

However, there are obstacles from my past that must be dealt with as well. Years ago I read *Healing the Masculine Soul*, a book by Gordon Dalbey. It was the first time that I was exposed to wounds from my past. It is still one of the most helpful books I've ever read. No one has had a perfect childhood, and there are no perfect families. Even God's first children failed in a perfect environment. Life isn't about perfection; it's about redemption. One of my favorite novels is *Les Misérables*. The irony of the book is that the character seeking perfection, Inspector Javert, commits suicide in the end. Everyone is going to suffer; everyone is going to screw up. Learning to suffer well and redeem the past helps to make a man amazing.

Now let's talk about obstacles from the past.

Obstacle 1: Insecure Attachments

Research has shown that our attachment patterns are set in early childhood and continue throughout our lifetime; the pattern is either secure or insecure. If a child grows up with caregivers who attach to them no matter what emotion they are experiencing, they will likely develop a *secure* style of attachment.

When adults with secure attachments reflect on their childhood, they usually feel that their mother and father were always there for them. They can remember events in their life (good and bad) in the proper perspective. As adults, people with a secure attachment style enjoy intimate relationships and are not afraid to take risks in love.

People who develop insecure attachment patterns did not grow up in a well-balanced, supportive, validating environment. Individuals with an insecure style of attachment often struggle to have meaningful relationships with others as adults. They will have to learn how to change their behaviors and patterns.

When people develop an insecure style of attachment, it can take one of three forms: avoidant, ambivalent, or disorganized.

- Avoidant – People who develop an avoidant attachment style often have a dismissive attitude toward emotions, avoid intimacy, and have difficulty reaching out to others in times of need. Many men fall into this category.
- Ambivalent – People with an ambivalent attachment pattern are often anxious and preoccupied. They will be viewed by others as needy because they require regular validation and reassurance. This is their recurring question: "Are we OK?" They feel insecure in relationships.
- Disorganized – People with a disorganized attachment style typically have experienced deep trauma or extreme inconsistency in infancy and childhood. They have no real coping strategies and are unable to effectively deal with

the world when overwhelmed. They are often moody and unpredictable.

People with avoidant or ambivalent attachment styles are generally functional as adults. Although they are not ideal ways of coping, these attachment styles do allow for some rational and logical approaches to deal with complex situations. But a person with a disorganized attachment style is often unable to process and cope with adversity. Soldiers with this style are often the ones who suffer PTSD.

The key to developing a secure attachment style involves reconciling childhood experiences and making sense of the impact your past has had on your present and future. You have to develop a coherent narrative about what happened to you as a child. In other words, you have to *explain yourself to yourself.* You also need to explore the impact it has had on the decisions you might have unconsciously made about how to survive in the world. You will need to think critically about how your early life affected your attachment style and work on breaking those patterns. We'll work on this later in the book.

Good news! Thanks to the *neuroplasticity* of the human brain, it will begin to change as you adjust ineffective behavioral patterns and beliefs in community with other men. A person who is insecurely attached can build the security he needs by practicing supportive and loving experiences in their lives. He needs secure attachments.

Obstacle 2: Unresolved Trauma

There are two kinds of trauma that we experience: trauma A and trauma B.

Trauma A is neglect. While trauma B is bad, trauma A is worse because you don't know what you don't know; you don't know what you're missing. If trauma B is getting what you shouldn't have, trauma A is not getting what you should have received. We'll expand on the blueprint or what you were supposed to receive in chapter 4.

Trauma B experiences are the bad things that happen to us. We suffer an injury to our body, our mind, our soul, or our emotions. Someone or something inflicts pain and suffering on us and there is an agonizing memory that still hurts. Whenever we remember it, we relive the pain of that moment. Here's one of my traumas that I had to work through:

> I was a pretty happy little boy, so my sisters say. Bold and fun is the way my sisters, June and Betty, would describe me. I was the sixth of seven siblings in the family. In a large family, there's always a lot going on, and I remember thinking, *Someone is going to explain all this to me someday!* I was wrong.

When I was eleven years old, someone I admired lashed out at me and belittled me. At that moment, I felt worthless and unloved. I was humiliated. My body quivered as tears ran down my cheeks. I crawled out of my chair and went into my room and closed the door. That night, I stood in the darkness of that room and said to myself, "Nobody's coming!" I also made a decision. "Nobody is ever going to do that to me again!" I was smart, and I would be strong.

In many ways, that was the beginning of me becoming an autonomous male. I would let people close to me but never close enough to hurt me—way too much pain there. I also became a warrior—a happy lion, but a lion with fangs nonetheless! Oftentimes, I defended myself, even from the people who loved me. I was still generally bold and fun. I had lots of friends and relationships, but I could be defensive and sarcastic when triggered. Years later, my kind wife, Linda, helped me process that pain. All I can say is it doesn't hurt anymore.

Obstacle 3: Masks and Triggers

❖ Amazing Men Don't Wear Masks

All of us grow up going to a masquerade party. We learn to wear masks. Amazing men learn to live without masks. They are transparent and spontaneous.

❖ Your Real Self

Consider this simple diagram:

SELF

SHAME

MY MASK

In the center is your real self. When you were born, you were uniquely you. Scripture says "you were fearfully and wonderfully made." You weren't perfect, but you were not terribly afraid of what others thought about you. You were "you."

❖ Shame

Look at the second circle. Surrounding your real self is a layer of "Shame."

This happens when someone spoke negatively into your life and your satisfaction with your real self began to erode. Something happened to make you feel ashamed. Shame is the opposite of joy. It means that someone isn't glad to be with me, as I told you in my story. In your own life, whether accurate or not, a realization began to surface that there was something wrong with you. You were made to feel as if you didn't measure up. You didn't measure up to the standards of your parents or siblings, the kids at school made fun of you, or you came to believe that you were inferior in some important way. Shame brought fear and fear caused you to hide. That's a problem! Because the more we hide, the harder it is to be known; we have to be known as we really are to connect at the most intimate level and to experience real joy.

❖ False Self

The outer layer is "My Mask."

To cover our shame, we consciously and unconsciously create a false self. This is the "character" we learned to play in the theater of life. We perform. Some of us learned that we only mattered if we were attractive, powerful, or skilled in some way. But each of us likely had an ace card we believed would make us lovable. Maybe you learned to be funny or you realized you were smart. You might have discovered you were athletic or good-looking. This probably took some time to reinvent yourself and put on the mask so that you were comfortable with it. But with practice, the facade was put in place.

There are two major problems with this false self.

- It's built on a lie. "I only matter if …"
- The real self is the part of you that gives and receives love. The rest is merely theater.

A mask is what you wear to be accepted. The problem is that in the final analysis, masks don't work. Your mask is not who you really are, and you can only receive love when it is directed to your genuine self.

❖ Triggers

What triggers you? Triggers come from old wounds that have not been worked through. When we're triggered, the past shows up in the present and people become problems. These old wounds cause us to write deep-seated commandments on our soul over time. My two big ones are "Thou shalt not bully me" and "Thou shalt not underestimate me." When I sense someone is doing either one to me, I can easily resort to little Johnny Bell and that's not good for anyone. I can become sarcastic and aggressive. Since I've become more aware of my wounds and talked them through with God and with my wife, I've learned to develop new—and more effective—responses. Now I can step back and take some deep breaths. I've realized that amazing men are not easily triggered, and they don't wear masks.

Before we get to the rest of the obstacles, we are going to take a detour in our next chapter and talk about maturity. I believe that insecure attachment styles and lack of maturity are two of the biggest problems in the world.

Questions for Chapter 2

1. The book says, "No one has had a perfect childhood, and there are no perfect families." What events in your past did this chapter bring to your mind? How are they obstacles to your emotional well-being and growth?
2. What insecure attachments do you think you may still experience? In what ways were significant people in your life not there for you?
3. Are your reactions to these obstacles typically more avoidant, whereby you shun intimacy, ambivalent, whereby you are anxious or preoccupied, or disorganized, whereby you lack effective coping strategies?
4. Can you identify major type A (experience of neglect) and type B traumas (inflicted pain) that you have experienced and still affect you today?
5. What does the book mean with "shame is the opposite of joy?"
6. In what ways do you feel shame?
7. What masks do you wear at times? What lies cause you to wear these masks?
8. What tends to trigger you? What unresolved wounds cause this in you?
9. Are you ready to move beyond these issues?
10. Do you have hope that you can become amazing?

Chapter 3

FIVE STAGES OF MATURITY

The Blueprint for Growth

Normal human development passes through a set of *stages* that can be identified as

- grace
- discovery
- justice
- sacrifice
- community

Grace – During the first four years of your life, your brain was looking for grace. You were searching for eyes that lit up when they saw you. You could have been upset, been frightened, or even have pooped in your pants, but someone (or more) looked at you with the eyes of heaven. You were a person of great value. And you didn't have to earn it. You were fearfully and wonderfully made. Every day was a new experience of being filled with joy. You felt special and you felt loved—unconditionally! Grace like that fills up a reservoir of joy and creates many roads back to joy.

Discovery – The next eight years of your life were about discovery. You were supposed to discover your true identity and how to do hard things. Your mom was likely the primary caregiver in your earliest years, but you needed a coach for this stage of life.

Dads were supposed to fill this role, but many of them didn't live up to the task. When this happens, a *father wound* will develop if nobody steps in to support you at that critical time. Thankfully, you can ask for help, or others can step in to sort out and heal the pain. You need to graduate from this stage by knowing what you're good at and how to endure hardship well. You should be able to "pack your own backpack and read a trail map."

Justice – As you enter adolescence, you are really entering adulthood. Your brain is looking for a group to belong to, and that group will be more important to you than your own individual identity. "Who are my people?" is the burning question of this stage. This is why the movie *The Breakfast Club* still resonates after all these years. Each student belonged to a group, even though they were mostly unhealthy groups. In this stage, you are supposed to learn about justice and being fair. You should be able to negotiate in such a way that everybody wins. After learning self-care and learning to take responsibility for yourself, you will be able to learn how to take care of at least one other person. You treat them the way that you would want to be treated; conceptual thinking enables you to practice the Golden Rule as you relate to others.

Sacrifice – The first three stages prepare a man for sacrifice. Marriage is the beginning of significant sacrifice and change. Nobody tells you that. When a couple says, "I do," they're really saying they accept the future sacrifice. They will never again be who they used to be. Singing a duet is much harder than singing a solo. Not every man will get married or have children of his own. However, every man will still need the motivation of sacrifice that marriage and parenting can bring; some men may become active godfathers to children of their friends.

Marriage is the kindergarten—the early years—of sacrifice followed by the parent stage. With children, the real schooling for parents begins. "It's a girl" or "It's a boy" means "I begin to invest everything I've ever owned into a miniversion of my wife and myself." And your children typically won't say thank-you. That's OK, because if you received grace, you can give it in return. An amazing man who is a parent can oversee and implement the first three stages for each of his children. He gives them grace, self-awareness, and skills and teaches them justice.

Community – The last stage of an amazing man's life is to be a grandfather or an elder. The types of things a father does for his children, an elder does for his community. An elder is always looking for people who are left out or injured—widows and orphans. Lots of people are abandoned in this world and an elder knows what to do about it. He delights in babies, coaches boys and girls, helps teenagers find a healthy group, and mentors others through the challenge of parenting.

That then is what it was *supposed to be, the blueprint.* You were designed to mature through all five stages with help from others. Emotional maturity is measured in relationships.

- When a man expects someone else to take care of his needs, especially his emotional needs, he is still in the infancy stage. Women who know him might describe him as an "emotional gold digger."
- When a man can't do hard things, can't ask for help, procrastinates, or is unsure about his unique identity, he is still in the child stage. Peter Pan is the classic example of the man who never grows up.
- When a man doesn't know how to bond with peers to form a group identity and doesn't know how to use his power wisely, he is not a mature man.
- When a man doesn't know how to give life without needing to receive in return, build a home, protect, serve, enjoy, and mature others, he has failed to become an emotionally mature parent.
- When a man lacks hospitality, doesn't know how to build community, isn't panic proof, isn't transparent and spontaneous, and doesn't know how to build trust, he is not an elder.

Nobody gets through unscathed, but you don't have to stay stuck. That's what this book is all about. I'm in the elder stage of my life. It wasn't easy to get here, and I couldn't have made it without going back to every one of the first four stages to see what was missing, address those issues, and rewire my brain accordingly.

The apostle Paul had it right when he wrote, "Not that I have already attained, or am already perfected, but I press on." By the way, I'm still working at it.

Questions for Chapter 3

1. The book says that normal human development passes through the five phases of grace, discovery, justice, sacrifice, and community. Where are you in this journey?

2. In your earliest years of life, did you have parents or caregivers who were filled with delight just to see you? If not, how has it impacted your life?

3. In your childhood, were you taught how to do hard things? If not, how has it impacted your life?

4. In your adolescence, did you have healthy groups where you belonged? Did you learn about fairness? If not, how has it impacted your life?

5. If you are in your adult and/or married stage of life, have you learned how to willingly sacrifice for others? If not, what stands in your way of practicing this?

6. If you are in your grandfather and/or elder stage, have you learned how to effectively care for the needs of the community? Are you engaged in "looking for lost ones: orphans and widows" who you can come alongside of and support? If you are not doing that, how can you begin?

Chapter 4

THE OBSTACLE COURSE

Part 2
The Present

In chapter 2, we looked back; now let's look around. When I look around at the world of men today, I see that we have a lot of work to do. However, I am encouraged because when I talk to other men, they want to get better. "Who doesn't want to be amazing?" But wanting to be amazing is not enough. As my friend Dave says, "Hope is not a strategy." Let's look at two key obstacles that we as men face today.

Obstacle 4: A Shortage of Role Models

Neuroscience tells us that we have a heavy concentration of "mirror neurons" on the right side of our brain. The right side of the brain is the identity and character center of the brain. The right side of our brain doesn't learn with words. Words are too slow; the right side cycles faster than conscious thought. These mirror neurons reflect or imitate what they see. Babies essentially download the personality of their caregivers. But the downloading doesn't necessarily end when we are no longer infants; mirror neurons function throughout our life.

To be amazing, we want to learn and practice the following six new habits:

1. stickiness
2. inquisitiveness
3. grit
4. protective gentleness
5. magnetism
6. being inspirational

Ideally, we want each quality to be our automatic response to our environment when it is needed. We don't have time to logically think about it. Life moves too fast. In addition to learning new information and practicing it, we need to see it in other men. We need role models who demonstrate a new way to respond to life's varied situations.

The greatest role model ever was Jesus. He not only *taught* his disciples how to live, He *showed* them how to live. In Mark 3:1–5, we read,

> He entered again into the synagogue, and there was a man there who had his hand withered. They watched him, whether he would heal him on the Sabbath day, that they might accuse him. He said to the man who had his hand withered, "Stand up." He said to them, "Is it lawful on the Sabbath day to do good or to do harm? To save a life or to kill?" But they were silent. When he had looked around at them with anger, being grieved at the hardening of their hearts, he said to the man, "Stretch out your hand." He stretched it out, and his hand was restored as healthy as the other.

Jesus was angry and distressed and what did He do? He healed the man's hand. That was a new download for those men and modeled a new way to respond when deep anger arises: taking loving and effective action. Even though He was angry, He wasn't predatory.

That's what role models who are amazing men can do.

Obstacle 5: Lack of Genuine Community

You can't be amazing alone and you can't be amazing in a toxic community. Every man needs a group of men to be in the foxhole with him and who will call out the best in him. When we go through the chapter on stickiness, we'll discuss the art and science of friendship, but for now, let's consider three things about genuine community.

1. Genuine community reminds you who you *are* in spite of what you *do*. People in this community will not say, "John, you're such an idiot. Won't you ever get it right?" What they will say is "John, that was the wrong thing to do and as amazing men we don't do that. That's not who we are."
2. Genuine community will help you practice the six habits of an amazing man as part of your group identity. They will be your "band of brothers" fighting with you against mediocrity. Thoreau observed, "The mass of men lead lives of quiet desperation." A genuine community of men will never let that be true about each other.
3. Genuine community will help you tune out the two main lies of the radio signal from hell.

    • "You don't measure up!"
    • "Nobody cares!"

Sticky friends will remind you that God has already prepared good things for you to do and that you are in the process of doing them or being shaped to do them. Furthermore, you're never alone. God has promised to never leave or abandon you. And oh, by the way, you can call sticky friends on your best day or your worst day. You'll develop intimacy and transparency with God, with your band of brothers, and with your wife and family.

Now that we've talked about the obstacles, let's define the *six dimensions of an amazing man.*

Questions for Chapter 4

1. Can you identify men in your life who model the six habits of amazing men: stickiness, inquisitiveness, grit, protective gentleness, magnetism, and being inspirational? How do they serve as a model for you?
2. Are you working on these habits so that they become reflexive or second nature to you, without needing to think about how to respond to circumstances?
3. Do you have a group of men, a *band of brothers*, who remind you of who you are and call out the best in you? If not, what do you need to do to find such a community?
4. Do you know the phone numbers of *sticky friends* who you can call on your best day or your worst day? If not, how can you begin to build this phone list?

Chapter 5

SIX DIMENSIONS OF AN AMAZING MAN

This short chapter will give the whole portrait of an amazing man in summary form. This is the view from 30,000 feet—the broad perspective.

The First Dimension – "How does a man connect with others?"

A sticky friend is a man who is able to enter and maintain a deep, transparent, trustworthy, reciprocal, loyal, mutual, and covenantal relationship with others over an extended period of time. Sticky friends will be spontaneous and bring joy to one another just by being together. They will see the best and bring out the best in one another. They will be brothers as God intended for brothers to be.

The Second Dimension – "How does a man navigate through life?"

An inquisitive student is a man on a lifelong journey to discover the truth and wisdom about himself, the people he is called to love and protect, the people who are draining or predatory, as well as to discover the answers to life in general. Sometimes we call this "connecting the dots" or "putting the puzzle together so that every piece fits."

The Third Dimension – "How does a man win the battles of life?"

> A warrior with grit is a man who accepts the reality that life has challenges to overcome, mountains to climb, and battles to win. Grit means maintaining hope and vision to change, even under the most challenging circumstances. A man with grit wins even when he loses because he learns from the experience. He bounces back. He can't be beaten because he won't quit. Grit is firmness of character, an indomitable spirit, and resilience.

The Fourth Dimension – "How does a man lead?"

> A gentle protector is a leader who has learned to protect others. He skillfully wields power to cultivate emotional maturity, promote a strong group identity, and increase productivity through trust, joy, and engagement. When an amazing man uses his strength the right way, people will thrive, have greater capacity, and develop their unique skills. Everyone has the potential to flourish.

The Fifth Dimension – "How does a man relate to women, especially his wife?"

> A magnetic lover is a man who loves and leads his wife, who continually seeks to understand her and helps her sort things out, who practices the three kinds of love appropriately with her, who makes her safe and secure, who romances her for a lifetime, and who brings out the best in her. His magnetism grows so that he and his wife become one in body, soul, and spirit, reflecting the Trinity and the love of Christ.

The Sixth Dimension – "How does a man inspire others, especially young people?"

> An inspirational mentor is a man who breathes life into others, especially young people. He calls out the best in them, and his affirmation gives them confidence to try and endurance to persevere. He doesn't always tell them which road to take, but he asks powerful questions about the journey. He models relationship, joy, and the ability to endure hardship well.

You Were Meant to Be Amazing

I believe that deep in the core of men, we all want to be amazing. It's our primeval calling. But we also have to know that there is a conflict inside each of us. *We are born as predators, and we need to morph into our true identities.* If we are not transformed, we will give in to the urge to be friendless, clueless, feckless, ruthless, offensive, and lifeless. Don't be that guy. Instead, become *amazing*.

Questions for Chapter 5

1. In your own words, how does a man connect with others?
2. In your own words, how does a man navigate through life?
3. In your own words, how does a man win the battles of life?
4. In your own words, how does a man lead?
5. In your own words, how does a man relate to women, especially his wife?
6. In your own words, how does a man inspire others, especially young people?
7. This chapter says, "We are born as predators, and we need to morph into our true identities. If we are not transformed, we will give in to the urge to be friendless, clueless, feckless, ruthless, offensive, and lifeless." What is your response to this?

Chapter 6
HOW A MAN CONNECTS TO OTHERS

A man of many companions may be ruined,
but there is a friend who sticks closer than a brother.
—Proverbs 18:24

We were made for bonded, intimate relationships. It's how God designed our brains. One of the worst forms of punishment is solitary confinement. That being said, relationships are still hard. They are also revealing. If you want to know what a man is like, try having a relationship with him. Stickiness is required. Stickiness is the ability to attach to others and, for the most part, stay bonded.

Stickiness and Joy Strength

How stickiness was lost. The "fall" in Genesis 3 affected our brain in two ways.

1. **The Left Side Damage**
   The left side of our brain is still able to reason and explain, but it denies the obvious—that God is the Creator, Judge, Ruler, Redeemer, and Restorer of all things. One of the biggest lies in the world is that we're here by chance. When we don't know our origin, we are deeply flawed. We lose meaning, morality, and destiny. Life is futile.

Because knowing God, they didn't glorify him as God, and didn't give thanks, but became vain (futile) in their reasoning, and their senseless heart was darkened. (Romans 1:21)

2. **The Right Side Damage**

The right side of our brain was damaged in a different way. We became predatory and victimized. We are now wired to spot weakness, and we have learned to use that skill to our own advantage. We became people of fear instead of people of joy. We lost "nineteen relational skills"[1] along with the joy strength we need to meet the challenges and conflicts of life. As a result, we are traumatized by neglect and abuse.

We have all experienced trauma in some fashion, some more severely than others. According to Dr. Jim Wilder, trauma is anything that renders us less than what God has designed us to be. Trauma occurs when our pain is greater than our joy strength.

Dr. van der Kolk, mentioned earlier, is a well-known traumatologist. He writes that developmental trauma (trauma that occurs during a child's developmental years, from birth to eighteen) is a hidden epidemic in the United States and is a pandemic throughout the world. Its effects are fivefold.

1. It blocks growth and slows maturity, both spiritually and emotionally.
2. It affects relationships, creating difficulties in attaching to others.
3. There is a loss of personal identity.
4. It causes the inability to regulate emotions.

---

[1] *The Lifeboat in Your Brain* by Chris Coursey (downloadable pdf).

5. Both learning and attention are affected. These types of problems, which begin in childhood, can be exacerbated as adults unless there are appropriate and skilled intervention and healing.

The Healing of the Left Brain

When our relationship with God is healed, the left side of our brain acknowledges the obvious fact that God is the Creator and Ruler of everything, and our minds begin to reason and explain from this understanding. We discover where we came from, why we're here, how to live while we're here, and our eternal destiny. You learn that you were made in the image of God for meaning and purpose.

The Healing of the Right Brain

The healing of the right brain is different. It's the healing of relationships. The right side has to be taught, in communion with God and a joy filled community, how the nineteen relational skills function and how to build joy strength. Joy strength comes from exercising your relational brain circuits. The more you exercise, the stronger you become and the more joy you have. The more joy you have, the stickier you become.

If you want a joy-filled life, you must build the habits that create joy. Habits are extremely powerful. One bumper sticker read, "The one who dies with the best habits wins!"

From a brain science perspective, a habit forms through repetition. The more often you practice something, the more quickly your brain learns to see that activity as normal. Within thirty days, your brain will begin to rewire itself to adapt to this new normal. If your new habit extends to sixty or ninety days, new pathways in your brain can become fully formed and habits established. It can take up to 254 days. Much like a reflex, they begin to happen almost automatically. You know that a habit has been created when you begin doing things without consciously thinking about them.

Habits are the practices that mold our lives and set the course for whether we will live with joy or with fear.

It starts with an understanding of how relational skills are learned.

Step 1 Is Acquisition

Relational skill acquisition requires a high-joy relationship environment. In the presence of this secure bond with people we admire, we will actually allow our brains to become like them and copy how they live. Bonds form and deepen in an environment of *hesed*, also known as "sticky love." Hesed is the kind of strong attachment to others that no matter what they do or how many times they do it, we still want to be with them. We might call it love, but this kind of attachment is more like being permanently glued to someone. God is described as hesed 249 times in the Old Testament. In the New Testament, the word *agape* is used as a translation of the Hebrew hesed. First Corinthians 13:4–7 is a good description of the sticky love known as hesed.

> Love is patient and is kind. Love doesn't envy. Love doesn't brag, is not proud, doesn't behave itself inappropriately, doesn't seek its own way, is not provoked, takes no account of evil; doesn't rejoice in unrighteousness, but rejoices with the truth; bears all things, believes all things, hopes all things and endures all things. Love never fails.

It's the sort of love you can't shake off. It sticks to you through every high and low, every success and failure, every malfunction and sin. It's the kind of love that we are supposed to have for each other and even, as a matter of fact, for our enemies.

Step 2 Is Practice

Practice is like going to a relational gym and working out. Practice does not require bonded relationships. Practice does not require someone who possesses the skills we are working on. We can practice with our peers and with strangers. Our friends who are sticky are there to help us when we're stuck and encourage the new practice. Even difficult people give us an opportunity to hone new relational skills. I remember golfing with a grumpy old man named Cyril. Over eighteen holes, I played golf while working to keep my relational circuits on. The golf was easy; Cyril was a challenge. He was a charming predator. Practice requires the least relational commitment of any element of relational skill development. Every day presents fresh opportunities to practice this skill. Negative emotions are always showing up—anger, fear, sadness, disgust, shame, and/or despair. Can you stick with people when these emotions surface in you or in them?

Step 3 Is Motivation

Staying motivated is the most relationally taxing part of developing relational skills. Why? Because we wear down over time and we lose our relational air. We can know and learn skills intellectually but never actually use them in real life because we are not always motivated to be kind, love our enemies, forgive those who hurt us, endure hardships patiently, and return good for evil. Motivation requires a huge relational investment compared to all the other elements of relational skill development. Relational skills that build character can only be transmitted where there is stickiness. Without the love that bonds us together, there is no lasting transformation.

Skills and Stickiness

No one is sticky all the time. For me, my brain gets short-circuited by problems, difficult people, and my own ego—mostly my own ego. Sometimes I know it's happening, and sometimes I'm oblivious. Whether I know it or not, my relational circuits shut down. I want the problem or the person to move to the other side of the planet. I stop listening and start trying to win. I become triggered and get stuck instead of being sticky.

According to Dr. Karl Lehman, here are some of the signs that we have shut down relationally:

- We don't feel like being around someone we normally like.
- We just want to make a person or problem go away.
- Our mind is locked on to something upsetting.
- We become aggressive in the way we interrogate, judge, or fix people.
- We don't want to make eye contact.
- We feel like it is the other person's fault if they are hurt by something we do or say.

Stickiness without relational skills is an agonizing story of people who care for each other but can't stop hurting one another. Relational skills without stickiness make people manipulative or clever predators. Education, power, spiritual gifts, or intelligence cannot produce stickiness or relational skills. Further, stickiness and relational skills work best in tandem.

This is the reason why God must be an active part of your becoming an amazing man. God provides the guidance, models the missing relational skills, and forms the foundation of the extended relational stickiness needed to create motivation. Neither God alone nor people alone will be sufficient. In the Garden, Adam had God, but he needed Eve as well.

We imitate what we see in the people who we admire. As God

heals us, we are better able to love and download our joy strength to others for God to speak into their lives. The most wonderful part of being in a healing, redemptive community is that God can actually rewire our faulty thinking patterns through the community's loving acceptance. As we look into the eyes of someone and show that we are glad to be with them, dopamine is produced and released in their brain and joy is downloaded!

The joyful community becomes a new family where God is our Father, and we become brothers and sisters. Healthy community rebuilds broken trust, where life can be seen as good and not bad. It also helps us learn to listen to God and to each other, building our God-given identity, and it encourages us to mature spiritually and emotionally, growing from childhood to adult maturity.

All of this produces in us our true identity. Mine, for example, is the following:

> I am, above all things, a man of joy, and the One who created me is always glad to be with me. He has created a community of men to gather around me. They will always be glad to be with me and I with them, so that we may model this, especially to those we join in their troubles, drawing them into God's kingdom. Our redemption and transformation have this single theme: *a return to joy, stickiness, and the spreading of the joy of our great King.*

Questions for Chapter 6

1. This chapter starts out with this proposition: "We were made for bonded, intimate relationships. It's how God designed us." Do you agree with this, and if so, why are intimate relationships so critical?

2. It also says, "We're hardwired to spot weakness, and we have learned to use that skill to our own advantage. We became people of fear instead of people of joy." What is your own response to this?

3. In the text, Dr. van der Kolk lists five effects of trauma. Which of these have you experienced, if any?

4. Did you look up the *nineteen relational skills* that were mentioned? Which of these are strengths of yours? Which are weaknesses? What can you do to build your relational skills?

5. Do you agree with the statement that "the more joy you have, the stickier you become?" If so, explain.

6. In the chapter, Dr. Lehman lists some signs that we have shut down relationally. Which of these are ways that you tend to shut down? Will being aware of these help you recognize more quickly when you are beginning to shut down?

7. "We become what we see in the people who we admire." How might you capitalize on this natural inclination to imitate others, especially in terms of choosing whom to spend time with?

8. Can you relate to the statement of *true identity* that concluded this chapter? How might you customize it to make it your own?

Chapter 7

THE ART AND SCIENCE
OF STICKINESS

Let's consider in this chapter the stages that friendships go through as they develop and deepen.

Stage 1 – Buddies

When does relationship happen? It happens as you live. You don't go looking for friends. That would be creepy. A needy person is looking for someone to fill them up and no other person can do that, except God. That's how codependency works, and codependency always ends badly for everyone. Genuine friendship never involves manipulation or threat. It is always a total exercise of your free will. In a friendship, either friend can leave the relationship at any time; you stay because you want to. That, in and of itself, is part of the joy of friendship. That is the freedom of friendship.

Think about it. How many choices are really that free? You didn't choose your family or your family traits. You were born into a whole set of circumstances that you had no say in whatsoever. You're surrounded by saints or by scoundrels, and they'll be with you for a long time. I love what Jay McInerney says. "The capacity for friendship is God's way of apologizing for our families."

I'm not saying families are bad. I'm just saying you have no choice in the matter. Families will always show up for weddings and funerals. At least one of them will probably help carry your casket someday. Proverbs 17:17 says, "A friend loves at all times; and a brother is born for adversity."

You may not like your siblings; they may not even like you. You may never imagine yourself socializing with them: meeting them for dinner, having a drink, or going on vacation together. But when the poop hits the fan, they'll show up. That's what they're born for!

But friendship begins when you cross paths with someone and a tuning fork in your soul goes off. It was a comment, a reaction, an understanding, or an outlook that told you and your future friend that you had something in common. You weren't looking for it or you might not have discovered it. C. S. Lewis wrote,

> The very condition of having friends is that we should want something else besides friends. Where the truthful answer to the question "Do you see the same truth?" would be "I see nothing and I don't care about the truth; I only want a friend," no friendship can arise ... There would be nothing for the friendship to be about; and friendship must be about something, even if it were only an enthusiasm for dominoes or white mice. Those who have nothing can share nothing; those who are going nowhere can have no fellow-travelers.

Ralph Waldo Emerson said of friendship,

> "Do you love me?" means, "Do you see the same truth?"— Or at least, "Do you care about the same truth?"

C. S. Lewis, again, wrote,

> Friendship is born at that moment when one man says to another: "What! You too? I thought I was the only one."

You and a potential friend could be coworkers, classmates, working out at the gym together, or sitting in the same pew regularly at church. Somewhere along the line, you discovered that you have something in common that no one else seems to get. With this, you have moved into the buddy stage. You may have nodded or smiled at the moment of recognition. This means you can laugh and roll your eyes together at some of the absurdity or delight that you both see.

Stage 2 – Self-Disclosure

Lots of men stay buddies for a lifetime. In fact, most men don't have true friends; they have buddies. They may play, drink, exercise, or even talk together. But there is the moment when a pair of buddies leaves the realm of buddyhood for the rarified air of true friendship and it sounds like this: "Can I talk to you for a minute?" or "Can I trust you with something?"

This level requires for one of the friends to be real and, at the same time, to believe that the other person is safe. This is the beginning of friendship.

Stage 3 – Reciprocity

Sociologist Beverley Fehr says,

> The transition from acquaintanceship to friendship is typically characterized by an increase in both the breadth and the depth of self-disclosure. In the early stages of friendship, this tends to be a gradual, reciprocal process. One person takes the risk of disclosing personal information and then "tests" whether the other reciprocates.

If reciprocity is missing, friendship never happens. You're back to being buddies.

Stage 4 – Intimacy: "Stickiness"

Once friendship is established through self-disclosure and reciprocity, the glue that makes it stick is intimacy.

The intimacy or sticky stage of a friendship is the artful part of the relationship. Only people who seem to possess a well-developed, intuitive understanding of the give-and-take that is required get to finish the dance of friendship.

The Bible boils it down to this: "Rejoice with those who rejoice. Weep with those who weep" (Romans 12:15).

People who know what to say in response to another person's self-disclosure will develop satisfying friendships. Key ingredients in doing this include

- emotional connection
- unconditional support
- acceptance, loyalty, and trust

It is also important *not* to start solving problems or offer too many opinions. Friends don't try to fix friends. Loving friends rarely cross that line unless invited. A friend with too many opinions about our marriage, children, or even our taste in movies may not be a friend for long.

That is not to say that close friends don't point out blind spots or wrongheaded thinking; they do. But they do it carefully; they use a scalpel and not a sword. The goal is restoration or prevention, not punishment and self-righteousness.

Proverbs 27:6 says, "The wounds of a friend are faithful, although the kisses of an enemy are profuse."

Nathan the prophet is a perfect example of healing surgery in rebuking King David (2 Samuel 12:1–14). He waited nearly a year and then used wisdom to help David see what he had done wrong. His careful handling of a very difficult situation brought healing to the entire nation.

Stage 5 – Best Friends

Overall closeness, regular contact, and genuine supportiveness are the things that maintain a good friendship and cause us to bond as one. But elevating someone to the status of best friend requires one more thing: group identity. Best friends are part of the same group. Our social identities are so important to us that we will do just about anything to reinforce this social view of ourselves—even go to war.

> The true soldier fights, not because he hates what is in front of him, but because he loves what is behind him. (G. K. Chesterton)

This is what it means to be "a band of brothers." Best friends are those friends who join us on a mission or cheer for us when we go! This is why friends living for the King and His kingdom can care so deeply about each other.

Stage 6 – Friends for Life: Deep Hesed

The bond between friends must be maintained over the years by the following four essential behaviors:

- continued self-disclosure
- continued supportiveness
- interaction (making the call or sending a text)
- honesty coupled with a positive attitude

I have a friend who is really good at this. One of his regular voice messages to me is "Hey John, it's me. Let's plan a time to catch up." Modern technology makes it easier than ever to truly stay connected.

Think of your investment in friendship as a relational bank account. Both friends have to put in relational currency. At first, one person may put in more than the other: perhaps a 60/40, 70/30, or even an 80/20 ratio. But there is no keeping score. First Corinthians 13 says, "Love doesn't keep a list of hurts or insults."

No records! And yet there's always money in the bank. How does that happen? It seems like sloppy bookkeeping. Here's how: even though there's no record, both friends trust one another to contribute to the relationship, and they do. Insufficient funds mean the friendship is over. Account closed!

Questions for Chapter 7

1. This chapter details the stages of relational development. If you were to count them, how many of your current relationships fall into each of these stages?
    *   buddies _____
    *   self-disclosure _____
    *   reciprocity _____
    *   intimacy/stickiness _____
    *   best friends _____
    *   friends for life _____
2. Are you satisfied with the number of relationships you have in these stages? What might you do to be more satisfied?
3. If you have few or no relationships at the deeper levels, what is hindering you?
4. Which of the keys to relationship development mentioned in this chapter do you need to improve upon (self-disclosure; emotional connection; unconditional support; acceptance, loyalty, and trust; bonding and commitment; supportiveness; interaction; honesty coupled with a positive attitude; keeping no record of wrongs)? How might you get started to make improvements?

Chapter 8

"BE INQUISITIVE": HOW A MAN NAVIGATES THROUGH LIFE

Amazing men are aware of the need to develop in the three realms of inquiry: relational, logical/rational, and spiritual.

- Relational learning is mostly downloaded from more-mature friends (on the right side of your brain) and makes you secure and mature.
- Logical/rational learning is a step-by-step process (on the left side of your brain) that can formulate a narrative for the past, present, and future for understanding, planning, and explaining.
- Spiritual learning is revelation that is given by God's Spirit and His Word that enables you to see the spiritual/invisible world and have the understanding and the power to be victorious and to rise above difficult circumstances.

Why Inquisitiveness Is So Important

Consider these facts:

- You don't know everything.
- If you think you know everything, it's worse than you think.

- If you admit that you don't know everything, you're on the path to wisdom.
- Jumping to conclusions is an ignorant way to live life.
- Asking questions is the best way to learn what you don't know in all three realms of inquiry.

Only a fool knows everything. A wise man knows how little he knows. (Shakespeare)

The ancients placed a priority on asking questions and seeking answers. The wisest man of his generation, Solomon, instructed students to search for wisdom and to set your heart on understanding (Proverbs 2:2–5).

Being inquisitive and curious along with asking powerful questions is the best way to navigate life.

EQ and IQ

Emotional Quotient (EQ) is the capacity one has to overcome the big six negative emotions in healthy and effective ways. With a high EQ, a person can stay relational whether they're angry, fearful, sad, disgusted, ashamed, or in despair. With a low EQ, one can become overwhelmed by these painful emotions and their relational circuits can shut down. They may react in ineffective, destructive, and even self-destructive ways.

Intelligence Quotient (IQ) is the ability to learn and use one's reason and logic to solve problems. With a high IQ, one is very good at solving problems through learning and rational thought. With a low IQ, one is not skilled at solving problems through learning and reasoning. For example, a high IQ might allow one to learn to analyze and strategize in an efficient manner while a lower IQ would make it more difficult and frustrating.

Now this is important: *EQ overrides IQ.* High-IQ people

who repeatedly make the same relational mistakes and eventually sabotage their own lives are all too common in life.

Let's begin by focusing on EQ and spiritual discernment. EQ is what the ancients referred to as spiritual discernment or godly wisdom. This is so clearly seen in the life of Jesus. Jesus was extremely emotionally intelligent. He was the most joyful man who ever lived. He perceived things with His Spirit rather than reacting to His circumstances or other people. He possessed an eternal perspective as He interacted with others and went about His Father's business. His primary methods were to ask questions and to continually interact with God.

We will examine the method of Jesus as well as three other amazing men who used questions and exercised emotional intelligence. We'll start with an amazing young man we meet in the scriptures.

❖ Joseph

Joseph was thrown into prison for a crime he didn't commit. His master's wife had tried to seduce him, but he refused her advances and physically escaped her clutches. Unfortunately for Joseph, she grabbed his coat before he could get away. She was so angry because Joseph wouldn't give in to her seduction that she accused him trying to rape her. Joseph was thrown into prison.

Even though he had every reason to be angry or depressed, Joseph continued to be emotionally and spiritually mature while he was in prison. Observing this, the warden in charge of the prison came to deeply respect Joseph. Just like his work and administration in Potiphar's home, Joseph was put in charge of everything in the prison. The warden no longer worried about anything because Joseph was successful in everything that he did.

While Joseph was in prison, two other important men were thrown into jail with him.

After these things, the butler of the king of Egypt and his baker offended their lord, the king of Egypt. Pharaoh was angry with his two officers, the chief cupbearer and the chief baker. He put them in custody in the house of the captain of the guard, into the prison, the place where Joseph was bound. The captain of the guard assigned them to Joseph, and he took care of them. They stayed in prison many days. (Genesis 40:1–4)

While in prison, the cupbearer and baker had a dream on the same night. The men didn't understand what their dreams meant, and it bothered them. When Joseph saw them the next morning, he noticed that they both looked upset and asked them what was wrong.

They said to him, "We have dreamed a dream, and there is no one who can interpret it."

Joseph said to them, "Don't interpretations belong to God? Please tell it to me."

The chief cupbearer told his dream to Joseph, and said to him, "In my dream, behold, a vine was in front of me, and in the vine were three branches. It was as though it budded, it blossomed, and its clusters produced ripe grapes. Pharaoh's cup was in my hand; and I took the grapes, and pressed them into Pharaoh's cup, and I gave the cup into Pharaoh's hand."

Joseph said to him, "This is its interpretation: the three branches are three days. Within three more days, Pharaoh will lift up your head, and restore you to your office. You will give Pharaoh's cup into his hand, the way you did when you were his cupbearer. But remember me when it is well

> with you. Please show kindness to me, and make mention of me to Pharaoh, and bring me out of this house. For indeed, I was stolen away out of the land of the Hebrews, and here also I have done nothing that they should put me into the dungeon." (Genesis 40:8–15)

Joseph paid attention to the men's facial expressions. Then he used his emotional intelligence and his spiritual discernment to give the meaning of the cupbearer's dream. Things would turn out very well for the cupbearer; soon he would be out of prison serving Pharaoh once again. Joseph asked the cupbearer to remember him when he was out of prison. Joseph wanted the cupbearer to ask Pharaoh to set him free because he was innocent.

There was still one more dream.

> When the chief baker saw that the interpretation was good, he said to Joseph, "I also was in my dream, and behold, three baskets of white bread were on my head. In the uppermost basket there were all kinds of baked food for Pharaoh, and the birds ate them out of the basket on my head." (Genesis 40:16–17)

Again, God let Joseph know exactly what the dream meant. Things were not going to go well for the baker. It must have been hard for Joseph to tell this bad news to the baker, but he told him the truth. Joseph told the baker that in three days, Pharaoh was going to order that he be killed and hang his body for everyone to see.

Once again, Joseph used spiritual discernment to know exactly what was going to happen. Knowing that Pharaoh would execute the baker, Joseph did not ask the baker to put in a good word for him.

Joseph used questions, his EQ, and his interaction with God to grow into an amazing man.

❖ Solomon

One of the most famous examples of the wisdom of Solomon is seen in the EQ tactic he used to resolve a seemingly unsolvable dispute in 1 Kings 3:16–28. The narrative tells of two women who came before King Solomon, bringing with them a single baby boy. They both claimed to be the mother.

The two women had both recently given birth to sons and they lived together in the same house. During the night, one of the infants was smothered and died. The woman whose son had died switched her dead baby with the baby of the other woman as she slept. The other woman, seeking justice, took the matter before the king. She stated her case.

> "Oh, my lord, I and this woman dwell in one house. I delivered a child with her in the house. The third day after I delivered, this woman delivered also. We were together. There was no stranger with us in the house, just us two in the house. This woman's child died in the night, because she lay on it. She arose at midnight, and took my son from beside me, while your servant slept, and laid it in her bosom, and laid her dead child in my bosom. When I rose in the morning to nurse my child, behold, it was dead; but when I had looked at it in the morning, behold, it was not my son, whom I bore. The other woman said, "No; but the living one is my son, and the dead one is your son." The first one said, "No; but the dead one is your son, and the living one is my son." They argued like this before the king.

Solomon could not tell from their words which woman was telling the truth. Instead, he issued a shocking command.

> "Get me a sword." So they brought a sword before the king. The king said, "Divide the living child in two, and give

half to the one, and half to the other." Then the woman whose the living child was spoke to the king, for her heart yearned over her son, and she said, "Oh, my lord, give her the living child, and in no way kill him!" But the other said, "He shall be neither mine nor yours. Divide him." Then the king answered, "Give her (the one who wanted to save the child's life) the living child, and definitely do not kill him. She is his mother."

Why would Solomon give such an outrageous command? Did he really intend to cut a baby in half with a sword? The narrative is clear that Solomon's intention was to discover the truth. He did so by watching the responses of the two women and relying on the maternal instincts of the true mother.

Solomon, in his wisdom, avoided the destruction of the baby and pronounced a true judgment, based on his profound knowledge of human nature (EQ).

❖ Daniel

King Nebuchadnezzar of Babylon ruled from 605 to 562 BC and greatly expanded the Babylonian Empire, conquering Jerusalem and deporting the Jewish inhabitants in the process. Daniel was one of those deported from Israel and granted an education in the king's palace.

One night Nebuchadnezzar awoke frightened by a dream. The king called for his magi to interpret the nightmare. This was standard procedure in a culture that placed a high importance on dreams and their meaning. However, he added an unprecedented requirement.

Not only did the royal wise men have to provide the interpretation of the dream, they had to recount the dream itself. The penalty for failure was death; the life of every magician, enchanter, sorcerer, and astrologer in the kingdom stood in jeopardy. (Daniel 2:5)

In contrast to the king who was predatory, Daniel acted with wisdom and tact when he learned of the king's decree. Innocent of any crime and confronted with death, there was no panic, no despair, no frustration but only wise words in response to the commander of the king's guard.

> So the decree went out, and the wise men were to be slain. They sought Daniel and his companions to be slain. Then Daniel answered with discretion and wisdom to Arioch the captain of the king's guard, who had gone out to kill the wise men of Babylon. He answered Arioch the king's captain, "Why is the decree so urgent from the king?" Then Arioch made the thing known to Daniel. Daniel went in, and desired of the king that he would appoint him a time, and he would show the king the interpretation. (Daniel 2:13–16)

Daniel asked questions and then interacted with God. He had his friends pray as well. He received the interpretation and gave it to the king. His grace under fear and duress saved many lives, including his own.

❖ Jesus

After the birth of Jesus, we read,

> When they had accomplished all things that were according to the law of the Lord, they returned into Galilee, to their own city, Nazareth. The child was growing, and was becoming strong in spirit, being filled with wisdom, and the grace of God was upon him. (Luke 2:39–40)

Early in his life, He was "filled with wisdom and the grace of God was on Him." Next, when we see Him at twelve years of age, we are told about one of the powerful ways that He attained wisdom (EQ).

> His parents went every year to Jerusalem at the feast of the Passover. When he was twelve years old, they went up to Jerusalem according to the custom of the feast, and when they had fulfilled the days, as they were returning, the boy Jesus stayed behind in Jerusalem. Joseph and his mother didn't know it, but supposing him to be in the company, they went a day's journey, and they looked for him among their relatives and acquaintances. When they didn't find him, they returned to Jerusalem, looking for him. After three days they found him in the temple, sitting in the middle of the teachers, both listening to them, and asking them questions. All who heard him were amazed at his understanding and his answers. (Luke 2:41–47)

This was how Jesus went through life. One day He met a woman as she approached a well in Samaria and He opened a conversation by asking her for a drink. Then He said to her,

> "If you knew the gift of God, and who it is who says to you, 'Give me a drink,' you would have asked him, and he would have given you living water." (John 4:10)

But she knew neither the gift nor the speaker, so Jesus proceeded. He knew she needed living water and introduced her to that need.

This was not unusual for Jesus. We read in the previous chapter that while a teacher of the law, Nicodemus, *felt* no need for a new birth, Jesus knew his need. The needs people have are not always the needs they feel, and what Jesus offers is not a feeling of satisfaction for a felt need but genuine satisfaction of a real need.

Jesus offered the Samaritan woman living water to quench her thirst. He used "living water" as a metaphor for eternal life. However, understanding it literally as "running water," she challenged his offer. "Sure, I'll take that water. Then I won't have to haul it again." The woman didn't want the water Jesus offered because she didn't perceive her own spiritual thirst. So Jesus asked about her husband. Why? She had tried one man after another and had not found satisfaction. She had attempted to quench a deep thirst for the *heavenly* with the *earthly*.

When she understood her thirst, she understood that Jesus was speaking metaphorically.

> "Sir, I perceive that you are a prophet. Our fathers worshiped in this mountain, and you Jews say that in Jerusalem is the place where people ought to worship." (John 4:19–20)

While she was only beginning to see who Jesus is, she did understand that an offer of living water was an offer of access to God. Yet there was still a barrier. How could a Jew make her a legitimate offer of access to God when Jews at that time did not believe Samaritans could come to God? Jesus had enabled her to see her need. He also overcame her objection.

The woman had asked,

> "How is it that you, being a Jew, ask for a drink from me, a Samaritan woman?" (For Jews have no dealings with Samaritans.) (John 4:9)

> "So where do you get that living water? Are you greater than our father, Jacob?" (John 4:11–12)

But Jesus answered none of her questions. He was not unresponsive to her inquiries, but He refused to be sidetracked by them. Instead, He focused on helping her see her thirst. Only after she saw her thirst did He answer her objection.

Earlier Jesus had engaged Nicodemus in this way. Nicodemus twice responded to Jesus's message by asking how such things could be (John 3:4, 9).

Jesus did not answer *how*. Instead, He insisted on the leader's need of the new birth. He knew that once Nicodemus saw the need, the *how* would not be an issue.

Jesus employs questions and demonstrates perfect emotional intelligence. Twenty years ago, John Marshall, bishop of Burlington, Vermont, compiled a book titled *But Who Do You Say I Am?* He collected and listed all the questions Jesus asked in the Gospels. He listed one hundred questions. Jesus's questions were not just to attain information but also to synchronize with the person He was talking to, in order to clarify where the person was coming from.

While your IQ is mostly fixed throughout your life, that is certainly not true about your EQ. In the next chapter, we'll discuss some ideas on how to increase your EQ and to be more inquisitive.

Questions for Chapter 8

1. Of the three realms of inquiry-relational, logical/rational, and spiritual—which are you strongest in, and which are you weakest in?

2. This chapter introduces the term emotional quotient. (EQ) What does this mean to you?

3. Which do you think you are stronger in: your EQ or your IQ?

4. The chapter says, "EQ overrides IQ." Do you agree, and if so, why?

5. What did you observe in the stories of the biblical characters Joseph, Solomon, Daniel, and Jesus that you might be able to emulate?

Chapter 9

BECOMING MORE INQUISITIVE

My father was a quiet man. He could sit in the room with you for an hour and never feel the need to say a word. But just because he was quiet didn't mean that he wasn't paying attention. He was a careful observer of life and knew what was going on even when we kids didn't think he knew. After I became an adult, I said to him once, "Dad, you'd be amazed at some of the things I did that you didn't know about." He responded, "Son, you'd be amazed at the things I knew you were doing."

I always knew when something piqued his interest. He would turn his head slightly and there would be a twinkle in his eye. Then he would say, "Hey feller (fella), how exactly does that work?" He always wanted to know how something worked.

My mother was the opposite in many ways. She had a hungry mind for books. She had many questions, and she pursued the answers in reading. She gave birth to seven children, and when any of us finished a book from school, we would pass it along to her and she would read it to the end. I remember in high school reading *War and Peace* by Leo Tolstoy. Halfway through, my mother said, "Aren't you finished yet?" She couldn't wait to get her hands on it. My sister, June, found her reading once at 1:00 a.m. She was seventy-three years old!

I come from parents who were curious about life, so asking questions has never been an issue for me. I once thought that everyone must have liked to raise their hand in class, but I've since learned that not everyone does. If you're afraid to ask a dumb question, you'll never know what you don't know. They say that there are no dumb questions, but I am living proof that there are. I asked more than my share of dumb questions. Thankfully, it never stopped me from trying again. My desire to understand has always been stronger than my fear of being embarrassed. I owe my curiosity to my parents. When men don't develop curiosity, they limit their chances of becoming amazing.

You might be saying right about now, "That's great, John, but I didn't grow up in that world. How can I be more curious, inquisitive, and develop my EQ?" Now that is a powerful question.

Develop Your Curiosity

Our minds are designed to be curious. In fact, our brains love it. We often think that answers bring satisfaction, and there is some truth in that. However, the real fun can be in the exploration, the journey. I like to do the *Jumble* in the newspaper. The words are scrambled, and I have to unscramble them and then take select letters from those words to answer the question posed by the graphic. I can usually get the words, but I don't always get the graphic right away, so I'll lay it aside. The answer sometimes comes to me in the middle of the day or overnight when I'm not thinking too much about it. Whether I get the answer early or late, it's bittersweet because I know that I'll have to wait till the next morning for a new *Jumble* challenge. The challenge is where the fun is.

Doing "the Columbo"

Detective Columbo (search 1970s reruns) was a frumpy albeit savvy detective who always caught the criminal. His main tactic was asking questions and piecing together the answers. And just when the bad guy thought he was getting away with it, Columbo would stop in his tracks, reverse direction, and say, "There's just one more thing …" Without fail, his final *extra* line of questioning would trap the guilty party.

The first thing you have to know about life is that it's a puzzle and a mystery. Approach it like a detective. There are clues. You have to find them and then you have to put the story together. The most important story is the one that God designed for you. It's your story and you have to solve the mystery by asking questions. And then you have to be able to tell it in a clear, concise, compelling way. Knowing who you are will help you to be curious about others and about life.

Start with Your Story

The most famous of the Delphic maxims is "Know thyself," which was the first of three maxims carved above the entrance to the temple of Apollo at Delphi.

John Calvin began his treatise on Christianity and religion with this line: "Without knowledge of self there is no knowledge of God."

In the modern world, the question would be "What's your story?"

Your curiosity about others and the world around you will grow exponentially when you have that kind of clarity about yourself and you're OK with it. Knowing your story will help you take off the mask that you may have been wearing.

Why You Don't Know or Tell Your Story

1. I'm embarrassed about my story.

This roadblock assumes that everyone else has a perfect story. This assumes that those Christmas letters you receive each year are accurate portrayals of reality. They're usually not. If the family picture included with the letter were a movie, you would see joy mixed with sorrow and pain.

My parents were cotton farmers who came to Chicago in 1956. They both got jobs in factories even though that was the last thing they wanted to do. They had a teenager and three other children, ages seven, five (me), and one. We lived in apartments and a rented house until I was in eighth grade. I knew that my story was different from the other kids. I was OK with that. I identified with immigrants more than the people who had been in Chicago for a long time. I learned that when I left the threshold of my front door, I was leaving the South and going into the Midwest. There were people who tried to make me feel inferior, but I never let them. This is my story, and your story is your story. Don't let anyone take it away from you!

2.   My story is not interesting.

There are no boring stories—not mine, not yours. Things have happened to you and you need to talk about your history and do so honestly. The best stories are stories of redemption. There is redemption in your story. Find it. What was painful? Who hurt you? What was unfair? What were you saved from? What have you had to overcome? How could your life be different? Who helped you? What have you learned? What would you say to others? What questions would you ask them? You may not know it, but your story is your advantage, and people will love hearing it! (If you can edit and tell it concisely.)

3.   My past is very painful.

Pain and suffering are a part of everyone's story. Learning to suffer well is required. If you are keeping secrets, you're not suffering well. Pain is part of your story, but it is not your identity. You must put it in context. C. S. Lewis wrote,

> Mental pain is less dramatic than physical pain, but it is more common and also harder to bear. The frequent attempt to conceal mental pain increases the burden: it is easier to say, "My tooth is aching" than to say, "My heart is broken."

You don't have to broadcast your pain on a stage, but you need to tell some friends and family that you trust. Allowing others to speak into your pain will help you eliminate lies that you may have attached to the pain. And you will learn what you were supposed to learn. Remember you paid a lot for that education!

Freedom to Be Inquisitive

Once you can begin to explain yourself to yourself, there is no limit to what you can learn. You can ask all kinds of questions about all kinds of things and that will make you interesting—and amazing. It's like getting out of prison. It's a whole new world when you are no longer preoccupied with yourself. It frees up a ton of brain space.

When you are free to be curious, you'll find curiosity in three areas:

- people
- things
- ideas

People

Curiosity about people develops your EQ. My wife, Linda, is very good at this. She can engage anyone to tell her stuff about his or her life. I tell her she should be in law enforcement. Of course, she would always be the *good cop*. I often ask her, "They told you that?" Here's why they tell her: she's the world's greatest listener and she really is interested in them. She practices what is called *active listening*.

Active Listening

> So, then, my beloved brothers, let every man be swift to
> hear, slow to speak, and slow to anger. (James 1:19)

Active listening is listening that keeps you engaged with another person in a positive way. It is the process of listening attentively while someone else speaks, paraphrasing, and reflecting on what is said, without judgment or advice.

When you practice active listening well, the other person feels heard and valued. Active listening is the foundation for any successful conversation. Active listening avoids judging the other person as they talk. It also means that silence is golden. Sometimes as people are talking, they need to pause. That's OK. Active listening includes nonverbal communication. You listen with all of your senses and give your full attention to the person speaking (e.g., smiling, eye contact, leaning in, and mirroring). Obviously, you ask questions, but the questions are related to what the other person is saying. You paraphrase or ask for clarification. When appropriate, you summarize by saying, "Here's what I heard you say ..."

Think of yourself as a therapist who is being paid to listen. You listening to them is actually going to validate them as the following story illustrates.

> Benjamin Disraeli and William Gladstone competed for
> the position of the prime minister of the United Kingdom.
> These two leaders were both great men but couldn't be more
> different.
>
> Gladstone was brilliant, witty, and had the experience to win
> the election. He lost. In this election, it was how each man
> came across to others. Jennie Jerome, Winston Churchill's
> mother, had dinner with both Disraeli and Gladstone just

before the election. When Lady Churchill was asked what her impression of the two men was, she responded,

> When I left the dining room after sitting next to Gladstone, I thought he was the cleverest man in England. But when I sat next to Disraeli, I left feeling that I was the cleverest woman in England.

Disraeli had spent the whole evening asking her questions and listening intently to her responses. He wanted to know everything about her. Disraeli, who had mastered the art of making other people feel important, won the election.

Things

Curiosity about things makes you smarter and more interesting. I have a book entitled *The Way Things Work* by David Macaulay. Here is its description:

> From levers to lasers, from cameras to computers, this 384-page volume is a remarkable overview of the machines and inventions that shape our lives, amusingly presented with a large dose of Macaulay's wit and personality.

I wish I could have given this book to my dad. It would probably have been the first book he ever finished. As I said earlier, his favorite question was "Hey feller, how does that work?" That's how he was wired, and it made him so much fun to be around. He would never be caught dead saying, "Same old, same old." For him, every day was new.

He had the curiosity of a toddler. Life was an adventure and he wanted to explore it. He came from a large family that included six brothers. They were farmers, hunters, fishermen, and trappers. He even spent time ridin' the rails where he picked up a barbecue sauce recipe from some African American men that my family still uses. I asked him, "Dad, how did you get that recipe?" He said, "I asked them if I could have it."

When he retired, he bought twenty acres of land in his Tennessee birthplace. He and my mom built a home and bought pigs, cows, and chickens. He put up fences and barns, hunted and fished, and entertained his grandchildren. My children have fond memories and great stories from their many adventures with him.

God has made a big and beautiful world for us to explore. You can explore from the top of a snowy ski slope or from the depths of the ocean. You can build a barn, or you can build a computer. There is so much to learn about, and you should never stop learning.

Six years ago, I told Linda that she had cooked for me for forty-five years and I was going to give her a vacation. I had grilled but had never cooked. She graciously accepted and I took over the meal prep and cooking. I had a huge learning curve and a new appreciation for all she had done for all those years, but I loved it. The biggest challenge was getting everything finished at the same time. Thankfully, Linda stepped in to be my sous chef. We are a great team and I have become a fairly decent chef, if I do say so myself.

Ideas

Curiosity about ideas will not only make you smarter, but it will also increase your EQ. Ideas are the force behind historical movements and ideas come from people. The most important thing to remember is ideas have consequences. Most people are only aware of *what* happened. The real question is this: *why* did it happen? Nothing happens in a vacuum. Another book I have is *Ideas: A History of Thought and Invention, from Fire to Freud* by Peter Watson. Here is its summary:

> Peter Watson's hugely ambitious and stimulating history of ideas from deep antiquity to the present day—from the

invention of writing, mathematics, science, and philosophy to the rise of such concepts as the law, sacrifice, democracy, and the soul—offers an illuminated path to a greater understanding of our world and ourselves.

My father wanted to know "How does that work?" I always wanted to know "Why did that happen?" This is the philosopher's question.

In 1948 an English professor at the University of Chicago penned a book whose main idea resonates well into the modern world and into today's news headlines. The professor was Richard Weaver and his book was *Ideas Have Consequences.*

The main thesis of Weaver's book is that philosophy undergirds all of society. What we believe about reality *matters.* What we say or think is real *matters.* Language, and how we use it, is important.

In 1948 many intellectuals in Europe and America were left dumbfounded as to how such atrocities could have been committed by Germany in World War II. In the 1930s, Germany was one of the most literate nations in the world, so it wasn't that Germans were ill-informed or unintelligent.

The problem, as Weaver saw it, wasn't literacy or education; it was the kind of philosophy that was informing the German view of reality. Weaver believed that the root problem was the philosophy of *nominalism.*

Nominalism, as defined by Weaver, "denies that universals like man, woman, tree, house, etc. have a real existence." In other words, truth is what you want it to be.

As Weaver put it,

> The issue ultimately involved is whether there is a source of truth higher than, and independent of, man; and the answer to the question is decisive for one's view of the nature and destiny of humankind.

You don't have to know everything about everything. You should know a little about many things. This will make you a kind of *renaissance man,* and it will move you forward in becoming amazing.

Identity, Calling, and Assignment

As you live, your story will continue to be written with new chapters. It is vitally important to know the difference between identity, calling, and assignment. *Identity* is who you are. *Calling* is what you do best. *Assignment* is where you serve to live out your calling and identity.

Your identity does not change. Your calling changes as it matures and improves. Your assignments change many times throughout your life.

Identity is the engine, the driver, and the power for life. Calling is a railroad track, the direction of life. Assignment is where we are at any given time period, the destination for now.

Identity

If you have received Christ as your Savior and Lord, you actually have two identities: a hidden one and an observable one, your heart identity. Think of it this way.

Your Hidden Identity

The hidden identify is waiting to be revealed in eternity.

> For you died, and your life is hidden with Christ in God. (Colossians 3:3)

> There are no ordinary people. You have never talked to a mere mortal. Nations, cultures, arts, civilization—these are mortal, and their life is to ours as the life of a gnat. But it

is immortals whom we joke with, work with, marry, snub, and exploit—immortal horrors or everlasting splendors. (C. S. Lewis)

The average person on the street is never going to see all that you are in Christ. You are a new person even though you look like the person you always were. What they will begin to see is that you are not like most people and your response to things that happen is really different.

The Identity of Your Heart

Your true heart is who God designed you to be. Every heart is different because of the unique combination of the main characteristics of their hearts. My brother David and I were born to the same parents, but the characteristics of our hearts are different.

I am bold. My siblings remember that when I was between one and two years of age, my dad seemed unapproachable to them. One day when we were all together in the living room, I crawled down from my mother's lap and across the floor to my dad's chair where he was sitting all alone. Everyone froze and held their breath. I grabbed his pants and inched onto his lap. What happened next changed my sibs' view of my dad. As I leaned on his chest, he put his arms around me! My sister Betty told me that after that, Dad was not as scary, and they were not as fearful.

My brother, on the other hand, is cautious and mathematical. The first thing David asks is "What can go wrong?" He is meticulous in his processing and planning. He helped my dad build a small barn in which the lumber cuts would all be diagonal. He worked it out in a diagram and pretty much told my dad what to do. My dad followed his directions even though it forced him to be patient. David's patience meant that my dad ended up with a beautiful barn.

There are kind hearts, brave hearts, bold hearts, hearts that speak truth, hearts that seek righteousness, hearts that love justice, etc.

Knowing your heart is critical. The pain you experience can help you discover your true heart. Kind hearts are hurt by meanness. Brave hearts are offended by cowardice. Truthful hearts hate deception, and loyal hearts hate betrayal. All hearts will be hurt; they don't have to be traumatized. A faithful and loving community will help boys and men learn to live with their heart—their true identity. Discipline will help you care for your heart and maintain your true identity.

Calling

Your calling is why you are here. What you do every day, your daily choices, should be aligned with fulfilling your purpose or calling; otherwise, your life is not well lived. Your identity should be reflected in your calling.

I remember my dad taking me fishing. Fishing is not my calling; it's rarely even my assignment. As we sat in the boat, I started talking to my dad. After a few words, he looked at me and said, "Shhh!" For a moment, I was stunned. I waited a little while and started talking again. "Shhh" for the second time came from my dad's lips. As I sat there, I thought, *I hate fishing.* Nothing came out of my mouth for the rest of the time I was in the boat.

As I sat next to my dad in the car on the way home, he turned to me with a half smile and said, "John, you just keep talking; that's what you're really good at." I knew then what my calling was. I didn't know it was called a calling, but I knew that it brought me joy and satisfaction. I have been on that track my entire life. Once, after school, I even had to write on a blackboard, "I will not talk in class," five hundred times. For a fulfilled life, your calling needs to be paired with the right opportunity or assignment.

Assignment

We express our identity and calling through the various assignments of life. Your first assignment is to understand and develop your calling. Good parents, teachers, coaches, youth leaders, and friends can be invaluable to discovery and development. After that, and for the rest of your life, you should search for assignments that allow you to fully apply your calling.

I told you earlier about my brother David. He is thoughtful and reserved. He always does the research, and he is meticulous in planning and execution. He loves problem-solving and helping others. That's his calling. He studied education at the university and became a math teacher. After years of teaching math, he went back to school to become a high school principal. He was motivated to do something about the inadequate leadership in the high school. He felt he could fix the problem and help the students and he did. Now he works at a university training young people who want to become math teachers. He's had three different assignments but only one calling.

Your assignment is not your identity and it's not your calling. You'll have many different assignments over the course of your life, but they will all come to a conclusion. If you've lived well, your last assignment will take full advantage of your identity and your calling. It will be the best assignment of your life. Many men don't do well in later years because they thought their identity was in their assignment. When they lose their title or their responsibility, they lose who they are, and they feel lost. That's too bad because there is always an opportunity to express your identity and your calling. Your identity, your calling, and all of your assignments will be your story. Amazing men are not clueless; they know their story.

Questions for Chapter 9

1. Are you a naturally curious person? If not, how can you become more so?
2. What is your preferred style of learning: visual, auditory, kinesthetic (learn by doing), or reading/writing?
3. Are you good at asking questions of others? Do you typically ask questions about people, things, or ideas?
4. Are you a good, active listener others like to talk to and feel comfortable sharing openly with you?
5. What does the chapter mean when it says, "Curiosity about people develops your EQ"?
6. Are you able to tell your own story, concisely, without embarrassment or bragging, and interestingly? If not, would it be useful to you to script it out and run it by a close friend?
7. How do you explain the concept of identity, calling, and assignment? How does this help you assess where you are in life, what you're doing, and what you should do next?
8. What does the chapter mean when it says, "There are kind hearts, brave hearts, bold hearts, hearts that speak truth, hearts that seek righteousness, hearts that love justice, etc. Knowing your heart is critical. The pain you experience can help you discover your true heart"?
9. Have you ever written a one-page autobiography and reflected on your life's trajectory and the key things you've learned? Why not try doing it and sharing your insights in self-disclosure with someone who is a true friend?

Chapter 10

"BE GRITTY": WIN THE BATTLES OF LIFE

Amazing men are tender, but they're not soft. They have grit.

Grit is the relentless resolve to keep pursuing a desired goal, without giving up.

Grit is critical for success. After a great deal of research, it turns out that across all ethnic, socioeconomic, educational, and psychological demographics, "one characteristic emerges as a significant predictor of success ... grit" (Pamela Lee Duckworth).

Developing grit starts early. A boy needs to start developing grit at four years of age. An adult who can serve as a coach takes on the task of teaching a boy to do hard things. An infant has all of his needs met without even asking; grit isn't required. However, once infancy is completed, grit is required for maturity through all the other stages. Becoming a mature boy prepares you to become a man, then a parent, and finally an elder.

The first stage of grit is learning to take care of yourself. The boy who never learns to take care of himself will never have grit for the future. He will always feel inadequate and always need someone to take care of him. You'll never be able to take care of someone else if you've never learned to take care of yourself first. In our modern culture, a great number of boys are missing out on gritty lessons and not developing properly through this stage.

Gritty Lessons

1. Learn to imagine and explore. This is how inquisitiveness and grit work together. A baby's world is very small; a boy's world is filled with adventure.

When I was in the fourth grade, we lived in an apartment in Chicago on a busy street. One summer, my friends and I wanted to play baseball but we didn't have a field to play on. Next door to my home was a vacant lot. It was filled with rocks and weeds, but I saw it as a baseball field. I shared my vision with my friends, and we went to work. We pulled weeds and cleared rock. Then we borrowed small pillows and flour for bases and baselines from our mothers (without asking for permission; I was sure it would be OK). We had fun for the next two hours until the owner of the lot came and chased us away. Still, it was worth it.

2. Learn to do hard things. Grit requires that you develop the capacity to do things that you don't feel like doing, like taking out the garbage. Tom Landry, coach of the Dallas Cowboys, said this to his new players: "A champion is simply someone who did not give up when he wanted to." Learning to do hard things means that your brain has to override your pain. A corollary to this is "Do one thing every day that scares you." This was the advice of Eleanor Roosevelt, a model of courage and resilience.

Modern neuroscience confirms this practical wisdom. When we succeed at doing one scary thing a day, we actually build out the circuitry in our brains that supports our capacities of resilience and the trust in our own ability to cope with hardships.

Consider all the things that you used to think were impossible that now seem easy. I remember skiing for the first time in Colorado. Standing at the bottom of the hill and looking at the top of the mountain on the first day, I said, "By the end of the week, I'm going to be going off the top runs." I finished that first day on a ski run off the top.

3. Learn what is real. Imagination is a wonderful thing, but not everything you imagine is real. It's important to know where imagination stops and reality sets in. Reality bites. Grit depends on a healthy mix of imagination and reality. Imagination is constantly tested against reality. Imagination produces many failures, successes, and comparisons. We learn from our results. We learn to say yes to healthy risk and no to foolish thinking. It's good to dream, yet it's terrible to be a daydreamer.

4. Learn to work hard and play hard. For many people, competition is a dirty word, and of course, it can be. There is healthy competition and unhealthy competition. Healthy competition is good. It makes you better. Even when you fail, you can learn a lesson. Competition is one of the ways that you discover yourself and where you fit in the world. If you're an alpha male, you should know that. If not, that's great to know as well.

When my kids were growing up, I coached them in all their sports teams. As a coach, one of the things that you have to do is cut players. Some coaches dreaded doing it. I didn't. I saw it as an opportunity to help the player. This is the kind of thing that I would say:

> You're a great kid and it's been my pleasure to have you try out for our team. We can only keep fifteen players on the team, and we have to choose the best players. You didn't make the cut. There is one of two reasons that you didn't make the cut. You weren't motivated to practice and improve your skills to be better or this is not your sport or something

that you were made to do. Now if you think you can do better than you've shown, then work hard and practice, and try out again next time. On the other hand, if you have realized that this really doesn't suit you, find out what does. You are really good at something and when you discover it, you'll be filled with joy.

A corollary to this is to find out what you're good at. Everybody is good at something. Don't let anyone tell you that what you're good at doesn't matter. Some people are really good at showing up. They're faithful; they serve without applause. The world needs more of those people!

5. Learn how to set goals and make a plan. Whenever someone comes to me and asks for help, my first question is "Where do you want to be in five years?" My second is "Where are you now?" Then "What requirements and resources do you need to get you where you want to be?" Finally I ask, "What can you do in the next thirty to ninety days to get you closer to where you want to be?"

Life is mostly a game of singles with an occasional double or home run. My parents and Linda's parents mostly hit singles, but they hit a lot of them. It takes a ton of singles to develop grit.

❖ The Gritty Apostle

The grittiest apostle was Paul. His Jewish name was Saul. He was a man of unquenchable zeal who possessed an indomitable spirit. His early training was as a member of the supreme court of his day. He had *gritty preparation*. He was raised in Tarsus, a city on the northeast corner of the Mediterranean Sea. It was a very influential city and had one of the top three universities of that day. At the age of thirteen, he was sent to Jerusalem to train with the foremost teacher in Judaism, Gamaliel. Here's his account:

> I advanced in the Jewish religion beyond many of my own age among my countrymen, being more exceedingly zealous for the traditions of my fathers. (Galatians 1:14)

Paul also had *gritty application*. Paul's grittiness showed up in his training and his zeal. As someone trained in rabbinic Judaism, he was the early church's worst enemy.

> But they cried out with a loud voice and stopped their ears, then rushed at him (Stephen) with one accord. They threw him out of the city and stoned him. The witnesses placed their garments at the feet of a young man named Saul. They stoned Stephen as he called out, saying, "Lord Jesus, receive my spirit!" He kneeled down, and cried with a loud voice, "Lord, don't hold this sin against them!" When he had said this, he fell asleep.

> Saul was consenting to his death. A great persecution arose against the assembly which was in Jerusalem in that day. They were all scattered abroad throughout the regions of Judea and Samaria, except for the apostles. Devout men buried Stephen and lamented greatly over him. But Saul ravaged the assembly, entering into every house and dragged both men and women off to prison. (Acts 7:57–8:3)

Listen to his recollection.

> I myself most certainly thought that I ought to do many things contrary to the name of Jesus of Nazareth. I also did this in Jerusalem. I shut up many of the saints in prisons, having received authority from the chief priests, and

when they were put to death I gave my vote against them. Punishing them often in all the synagogues, I tried to make them blaspheme. Being exceedingly enraged against them, I persecuted them even to foreign cities. (Acts 26:9–11)

One of the most dangerous things for a warrior with grit is to be headed in the wrong direction. Saul/Paul was obsessed and believed that his obsession was right. He believed he was on a mission from God! Something dramatic would have to happen to turn him around and put his grit to good use. And it did!

Paul had the *grit to change*. On the road to Damascus, Saul was struck down by a blinding light. Saul heard a voice say,

"Saul, Saul, why do you persecute me?"
He said, "Who are you, Lord?"
The Lord said, "I am Jesus, whom you are persecuting. But rise up and enter into the city, then you will be told what you must do." (Acts 9:4–6)

Saul was blinded. They led him into Damascus to a man named Judas, on Straight Street. For three days, Saul was blind and didn't eat or drink. Meanwhile, Jesus appeared in a vision to a disciple in Damascus named Ananias and told him to go to Saul. Ananias was afraid because he knew Saul's reputation as a merciless persecutor of the church.

Jesus repeated His command, explaining that Saul was His chosen instrument to deliver the gospel to the Gentiles, their kings, and the people of Israel. So Ananias found Saul at Judas's house, praying for help. Ananias laid his hands on Saul, telling him Jesus had sent him to restore his sight and that Saul might be filled with the Holy Spirit.

Scales fell from Saul's eyes, and he could see again. He arose and was baptized as a follower of Jesus. Saul ate, regained his strength, and stayed with the Damascus disciples for three days.

Saul the persecutor is remembered as the apostle Paul, his Roman name, the first missionary of the young church. He became the most determined of the apostles, suffering brutal physical pain, persecution, and finally, martyrdom. He was a man with true grit.

❖ Grit Modeled in Paul

Courage

Courage is overcoming fear and managing vulnerability. John Wayne said, "Courage is being scared to death, but saddling up anyway." The same part of the brain that houses fear houses courage.

The apostle Paul, as great as he was, was not without his periods of doubt and fear. When he wrote 1 Corinthians, he informed the believers at Corinth that while he was with them, he experienced weakness, fear, and much trembling (1 Corinthians 2:3).

While Paul was at Corinth, the Lord spoke to His apostle in a night vision and admonished him.

> The Lord said to Paul in the night by a vision, "Don't be afraid, but speak and don't be silent." (Acts 18:9)

He literally told him, "Stop being afraid." The implication clearly is that Paul was struggling with fear internally at this time.

Here is a quote that I pasted to the inside back cover of my Bible more than thirty years ago. It has inspired and helped me many times. It's the man in the arena.

> It is not the critic who counts: not the man who points out how the strong man stumbles or where the doer of deeds could have done better. The credit belongs to the man who is actually in the arena, whose face is marred by dust and sweat and blood; who strives valiantly; who errs and

comes up short again and again, because there is no effort without error and shortcoming; but who does actually strive to do the deeds; who knows the great enthusiasms, the great devotions; who spends himself in a worthy cause; who at the best, knows in the end, the triumph of high achievement, and who at the worst, if he fails, at least fails while daring greatly, so that his place shall never be with those cold and timid souls who neither know victory nor defeat. (Teddy Roosevelt)

A Bias toward Action

The man with true grit doesn't just talk a good game. Besides dependability, he has a bias toward action; he is achievement oriented. An achievement-oriented man is one who works tirelessly, does his best, and completes the job. Besides being well prepared, Paul had *tenacity*, an undefeatable *determination of purpose* to do whatever he set out to do whether it was persecuting Christians or building up the church. Paul's life of overcoming adversity is an example for every man. At the close of his life, Paul summed up his life and work.

I have fought the good fight. I have finished the course. I have kept the faith. (2 Timothy 4:7)

Goal Setting

Angela Duckworth writes,

Achievement is the product of talent and effort, the latter a function of the intensity, direction, and duration of one's exertions toward a long-term goal.

The apostle Paul had the benefit of God telling him from the start His long-term plans for him.

> He (Paul) is my chosen vessel to bear my name before the
> nations and kings, and the children of Israel. For I will show
> him how many things he must suffer for my name's sake.
> (Acts 9:15–16)

Paul had a deep love for his Jewish brothers and sisters but understood that he was called to take the gospel to the nations who weren't Jewish. In accordance with God's plan, he set his goals in alignment with God's will. He wanted to take the good news of Jesus to places where it had never been heard. He wrote to the believers in Rome and told them of his great desire to come to Rome even though he had never met them.

Paul eventually made it to Rome as a prisoner. He was held for two years and then released. He continued his travels and his teaching, always working toward the fulfillment of his long-term goals. He was arrested again and sent back to Rome. Eusebius claimed that Paul was beheaded at the order of the Roman emperor Nero or one of his subordinates. Here's my summary of Proverbs 6:6–11: to live with no motivation or planning is not God's desire for you.

Resilience

Andrew Zolli defines *resilience* as "a dynamic combination of optimism, creativity, and confidence, which together empower one to reappraise situations and regulate emotion."

Paul was one of the most resilient men in the history of the world. He had to face things that would crush most men.

> Are they servants of Christ? ... I am more so: in labors
> more abundantly, in prisons more abundantly, in stripes
> above measure, and in deaths often. Five times I received
> forty stripes minus one from the Jews. Three times I was
> beaten with rods. Once I was stoned. Three times I suffered

shipwreck. I have been a night and a day in the deep. I have been in travels often, perils of rivers, perils of robbers, perils from my countrymen, perils from the Gentiles, perils in the city, perils in the wilderness, perils in the sea, perils among false brothers; in labor and travail, in watchings often, in hunger and thirst, in fastings often, and in cold and nakedness.

Besides those things that are outside, there is that which presses on me daily: anxiety for all the assemblies. Who is weak, and I am not weak? Who is caused to stumble, and I don't burn with indignation? (2 Corinthians 11:23–29)

Excellence, but Not Perfection

Trying to be perfect will only succeed in giving you ulcers, as well as numerous negative emotions. Anxiety, low self-esteem, obsessive-compulsive disorder, substance abuse, and clinical depression are only a few of the conditions ascribed to perfectionism. Paul knew that perfection in this life was unattainable, but that never stopped him from striving to be excellent. In 1 Corinthians 15:9–10, he said,

> For I am the least of the apostles, who is not worthy to be called an apostle, because I persecuted the church of God. But by the grace of God I am what I am. His grace which was given to me was not futile, but I worked more than all of them; yet not I, but the grace of God which was with me.

❖ Paul's Secret: Faith

Paul set goals, made plans, and achieved many things. In all this, he was courageous and resilient and he strived for excellence in everything he did. But he had a secret source of strength and grit.

> I can do all things through Christ, who strengthens me.
> (Philippians 4:13)

Faith is the secret to grit that won't disappoint or fade away. Did you know that we all have been brainwashed since birth with a false concept of the basis of human activity? We have been sold on the lie that we have in ourselves what it takes to be what we want to be, to achieve whatever we desire to be. We have an air of bravado that we have what it takes, or if we do not have it now, we know where we can get it. We can educate ourselves, we can acquire more information, we can develop new skills, and when we accomplish this, we will have what it takes to be what we want to be. These things may all be helpful, but they are not enough.

We on our own do not have what it takes, and we never did have. The only one who can give us the grit we need is Jesus Christ. He proposes to reproduce His life in us. Our part is to expose every situation to His power in us, and by depending upon Him and not upon ourselves, we are to meet every situation, enter every circumstance, and perform every activity. We cease from our own labors yet have everything we need to do every good thing that we have been designed to do. That's true grit.

In the next chapter, let's dig deeper into the element of faith and a special kind of grit: *spiritual grit.*

Questions for Chapter 10

1. "Amazing men are tender, but they're not soft. They have grit." What is grit, in your words? How do you personally live out grittiness?

2. The gritty lessons are learn to imagine and explore, learn to do hard things, learn what is real, learn to work hard and play hard, and learn how to set goals and make a plan. Which of these lessons are you still learning, and what will you do to become a man of amazing grit?

3. The apostle Paul lived a gritty life and demonstrated courage, a bias toward action, goal setting, resilience, and excellence without being a perfectionist. Which of these could you be better at, and what will you do to get there?

4. Paul was also a man of deep faith and confidence in his strength that came from Christ. What stands out for you as you read the section on "Paul's Secret: Faith"?

Chapter 11

Spiritual Grit

Three New Enemies

If you have accepted Jesus as your Lord and Savior, at that moment, your life actually got more complex and you required more grit. It's the kind of grit that comes by grace through faith. I call it *spiritual grit*. Without it, you'll never finish the work that God has prepared for you to do.

You may not have been warned, but when you accepted Christ, you made three new enemies: the *world,* the *flesh* (or *ego*), and the *devil.* Each of these will attempt to manipulate you to make you ineffective and fail in every area of life. You need to understand each one of their respective strengths and weaknesses as well as your own newfound strengths and weaknesses. Each enemy can be defeated but only if you know their tactics and who can help you be victorious. Time to meet your enemies.

Enemy 1: The World

What do we mean when we say "the world" in this book? We're not talking about the physical world or nature. We're not talking about the wonder of a sunrise, the forests, mountains, oceans, or the beauty of God's creation. God looked on His creation and said it was good. Even in its fallen condition, it still reflects His glory.

We should love this created world for what it is: a reflection of the glory of God.

Secondly, we're not talking about people.

> For God so loved the world, that he gave his one and only Son. (John 3:16)

What is the world that God so loved? It is not the inanimate world or even the animal kingdom; it is the human world. God so loved *people*. John 1:10–12 says that when Jesus came into the world that He had made, He was rejected by people, but He still loved them and gave His life for them.

Well then, if it's not the created world and it's not the human world, what is it? It is the invisible, spiritual system of evil. Systems are made up of ideas, activities, and purposes. The world is the evil system with all of its elements and all of its components that work against the things of God. It is the world that Jesus spoke of when He said,

> If the world hates you, you know that it has hated me before it hated you. If you were of the world, the world would love its own. But because you are not of the world, since I chose you out of this world, therefore the world hates you. (John 15:18–19)

At the very beginning, it wasn't that people on their own hated God; it wasn't that there was something about the created order that reacted against their Creator. The world that hated Jesus was the world of perversion, lies, false hopes, and crushed dreams.

Satan introduced sin to Adam and Eve, and sin became an organized, corporate system through their descendants: through families, neighborhoods, villages, towns, cities, states, nations, business, government, education, religion, arts/entertainment, and media. It infects everything and everyone. It is the basis for all of the false promises and lies of fulfillment that Satan uses to entice human beings. If Satan is the spider, the world is his web. The world is the enemy system that seeks to conform you into its mold (Romans 12:2).

Enemy 2: The Flesh (Ego)

When Satan fell from his lofty position, he came to God's newly created earth. He began observing Adam and Eve in the Garden of Eden. Adam and Eve had no awareness of sin or rebellion. They only did what God told them to do without ever questioning what He said. If Eve came to Adam and said, "What are you doing today?" Adam would say, "I'm going to till the ground to plant a garden" or "I'm going to name the animals." Eve might have responded, "Why are you going to do that?" Adam's answer would be "Because God told me to!" That's it. No more questions. No wondering whether it was right or wrong because they didn't know the concept of right and wrong. We were designed to do what God said. If we always did exactly that, everything would be perfect. God would only need to tell us what to do. The simple answer to why the world is broken is that we fail to listen and obey God's instructions.

Into Eden Satan came, and everything changed. In Genesis 3, he had been observing that Eve kept coming back to a tree that she was forbidden to eat from: the Tree of the Knowledge of Good and Evil. It was the only tree that was forbidden; there was abundant fruit throughout the Garden.

Satan slandered God, which he constantly does, and enticed Eve to violate God's command. Why did she do it? She wanted to be God, just as Satan did. The problem is that she was never designed to be in that role. After the deception and her fall, Adam joined her in the rebellion. He failed in his leadership role.

When Adam and Eve violated God's command, something internal and spiritual changed. The nature inside both of them, which had had a *favorable disposition toward God,* was put to death and replaced with a nature with a *disposition that was hostile toward God*. This replacement nature wanted to take the place of God in human life and be the master. This nature, in competition with God, is often called the old nature or the flesh. Most of the time when the apostle Paul uses the word *flesh*, he is not referring to the physical part of you. (Paul does not regard the body as evil in itself. That's a leftover from Greek philosophy.) This flesh referred to is man's natural predisposition to rule his own life rather than to let God rule. From here on, we'll refer to it as the old nature or simply ego.

The ego seeks to rule over a person in all affairs of life, good or evil. The ego wants control. The ego is in defiance of God even when it seems to be doing good things. Every baby, every human being, is born with this old nature. This old nature is passed down father to son and father to daughter.

The only human being to escape this corruption was Jesus because His mother was a virgin, and He was conceived by the Holy Spirit. As a result, His disposition was always favorable to God and He desired to do whatever His Father told him to do. He was born without an old nature or ego. In John 14:30–31, He says,

> I will no more speak much with you, for the prince of this world comes, and *he has nothing in me.* But that the world may know that I love the Father, and as the Father commanded me, even so I do. Arise, let's go from here.

The rest of us live in sinful ways when we follow Satan's counsel. Now let's discuss our third enemy.

Enemy 3: Satan or "the Adversary"

One of the major problems with our three enemies is that they are all doubted, denied, or downplayed in the skeptical world of men, especially in Western culture. This is especially true of Satan. At the same time, it would be hard to find a culture, society, or tribe that does not have some concept or fear of an invisible evil power. The personality behind evil in the world is Satan. The scriptures expose him as the creature who first corrupted humanity and our world.

In the second half of Ezekiel 28, we are introduced to a wise, beautiful, and powerful angelic being whose job was to protect God's holiness (verses 12–19). But he was lifted up with pride because of his beauty. His pride led him to rebel against God. Isaiah also describes his pride and his fall (Isaiah 14:12–14). Essentially, he wanted to be like God. He led a rebellion in which one-third of the angels in heaven (now called demons) joined him (Revelation 12:4). This Satan is also known as the devil, the god of this age, Lucifer, etc. He is the first enemy to be aware of and defeated.

The only one in all history who has ever consistently defeated the devil, not only in life but also in His death, is the Lord Jesus Christ. He exposed the strategy and the tactics of Satan when He said, "The devil is a liar and a murderer from the beginning" (John 8:44). The strategy of the devil is to murder. The tactic by which he accomplishes this is to lie and deceive. All he wants to do is destroy what God has made. His power is totally negative, completely destructive in every way. The only one who can defeat Satan is Jesus.

Defeating the Enemies

Our foes are three in number: the world, the ego, and the devil. Now this is important: each member of the divine Trinity has a specific role to focus on and a specific enemy to conquer.

- The world is the *external* foe—conquered by the Father.
- The ego is the *internal* foe—conquered by the Holy Spirit.
- The devil, or Satan, is the *infernal* foe—conquered by the Son.

It is wonderful to know that we have the all-powerful

Trinity—Father, Son, and Spirit—and all the forces of their heavenly army to defeat our enemies.

❖ Overcoming the World

There are only two kingdoms that you can be a citizen of: the kingdom of God or the kingdom of this world. Each one promises glory—the glory of God or the glory of the world. We seek either the glory that comes from men or the glory that comes from God. They are mutually exclusive. You will love one and hate the other or you will be devoted to the one and despise the other. You cannot serve two masters or their systems (Matthew 6:24). The apostle John put it this way:

> Don't love the world or the things that are in the world. If anyone loves the world, the Father's love isn't in him. For all that is in the world, the lust of the flesh, the lust of the eyes, and the pride of life, isn't the Father's, but is the world's. The world is passing away with its lusts, but he who does God's will remains forever. (1 John 2:15–17)

Love for the Father drives out love for the world and love for the world drives out love for the Father. As stated, love for the world is characterized by the following three things:

- lust of the flesh
- lust of the eye
- the pride of life

Lust is desire and these three desires are powerful, but they are temporary. The word for "life" does not refer to the state of being alive but to the things in the world that make life possible. The phrase "pride of life" means pride in livelihood, pride in what you possess—the things you have. The first two—lust of the flesh and lust of the eyes—refer to desires for what we don't have. The world is driven by these two things: passion for pleasure and pride in possessions.

The passion for pleasure is described in two ways because there are two large classes of pleasure: physical and aesthetic. The lust of the flesh involves bodily pleasures. The flesh here is not our ego but our physical hungers and desires. The lust of the eyes involves aesthetic and intellectual pleasures. Some people derive pleasure from a raunchy lifestyle and others from a sophisticated lifestyle. Some enjoy the bawdy tavern, and some enjoy the fancy nightclub. We covet these pleasures, and after we acquire them, we become prideful of our lifestyle.

So is the solution for lust to eliminate all desire as Buddhism teaches? No, God gave us desires: the desire for food, shelter, clothing, sex, beauty, music, relationship, etc. But He wants to be the source of provision for our desires. We must not look to the world to satisfy our souls; rather, we must depend on Him. He has promised to take care of us, and He does so, often through the family of God.

The ways of the kingdom of God are laid out in Matthew 5–7, called the Sermon on the Mount. An important part of that teaching is the Lord's Prayer, which begins this way: "Our Father in heaven …"

We recognize that He is over everything, in heaven and earth. He is holy, and His kingdom and His will need to come to the earth. The prayer is filled with requests for things that He has promised to give us: physical needs like bread, which is food, as well as spiritual needs like forgiveness, guidance, and deliverance. Then it closes with "Yours is the Kingdom and the power and the glory, forever and ever!"

Through faith we believe that He exists and that He will provide all of our needs. We trust in His promises. The more we focus on Him, the more the world loses its allure.

❖ Overcoming the Ego

Contrary to popular belief, this is the most dangerous enemy because it's the most subtle and insidious. This topic will be explored in depth in chapter 14.

❖ Overcoming Satan

Satan is a schemer. His tactics fall into two major divisions: he attacks people both directly and indirectly. He is capable of direct confrontation with human beings as well as a more deceptive, indirect approach. Through these two avenues, he and his demons maintain his worldwide control over humanity. The devil and his army are not visible. The devil's activity is in the realm of the invisible realities of life, the heavenly places. This is also where God works and is in charge.

Direct Confrontation

Satan makes a direct assault upon human life through his invisible army. This direct assault is what the Bible refers to as "demon possession": the outright control of human personality by the power of a wicked spirit. It also includes activities, such as soothsaying, occultism, spiritualism, and related black magic arts (e.g., astrology, horoscopes, voodooism, and fortune-telling).

Down through history, there have been outbreaks of demon possession described by missionaries in many lands. However, wherever Christian teaching spreads, the direct assault of these evil powers upon human life is kept in check. Jesus never cast out a demon in Judea, but He did so in Galilee and the Decapolis. Even secular teaching that is based on Christian values and is moral and uplifting has an ability to keep these manifestations under control. But when education becomes purely secular and dismisses God and His Word, reason and logic are not enough to restrain these powers. As our world grows increasingly godless and more and more secularized, we will find an increase of demonic manifestation creeping into our culture and becoming part of our so-called civilized life. The direct attacks of the evil one are defeated by calling out to God in fervent prayer (Mark 9:29).

Indirect Attacks

The apostles seldom mention the direct attack of Satan against human beings. The demons were stirred up by the Lord's presence on earth, but this faded away after He left so that in the epistles you do not get the same concern for direct demonic activity as you do in the Gospels. Most of the attacks of the devil are not direct but indirect. That is why they are called the *schemes* of the devil.

This indirect approach comes mostly through the other two enemies: the world and the ego, which we introduced earlier. The devil works behind the scenes to distort, to counterfeit, to masquerade, and to create illusion and fantasy.

The world as a human society blindly and universally accepts false values, shallow insights, and deluded ideas of reality. Then it insists on conformity to worldly standards.

The ego is also complicit because of that inward pull within us toward total independence, toward being our own gods and running our little world between our ears to suit ourselves. We have a continual urge toward self-centeredness and selfishness.

Now then, how can we be victorious over this powerful enemy? As we noted earlier, the only one who is able to defeat the devil is Jesus Christ. The apostle Paul tells us how to defeat this enemy. We are to put on the Lord Jesus Christ, and we are to put on the whole armor of God (Romans 13:14; Ephesians 6:11). Then and only then can we defeat Satan. In the next chapter, let's examine this armor and how to put it on by faith.

Questions for Chapter 11

1. When you first heard about Christianity, were you told only the *good* news? Were you also told about the lifelong spiritual conflict that you would be engaged in or about the new enemies that you would need to battle?

2. If you have experienced the spiritual battle, have you ever had second thoughts about your faith or felt like you had experienced a bait-and-switch? If so, have you since settled your feelings about this? If not, how might you address these feelings?

3. Which of the enemies—the world, the ego, or the devil—cause you the most difficulty? In what ways are you most troubled?

4. Knowing that you are partnered with the three persons of the Trinity to battle our three enemies, how does that give you comfort?

5. The chapter says, "Love for the Father drives out love for the world and love for the world drives out love for the Father" and "love for the world is characterized by the following three things: lust of the flesh, lust of the eye, and the pride of life." Which of these three are the most tempting for you? What might you do about it?

6. What stood out for you as you read the paragraphs of "Overcoming Satan"?

Chapter 12

SPIRITUAL ARMOR: PART 1

In Ephesians 6, Paul describes the following six pieces of armor:

- belt of truth
- chest-plate of righteousness
- shoes of the Gospel of peace
- shield of faith
- helmet of salvation
- sword of the Spirit

Each piece of armor represents a different aspect of Christ. When we put on this armor, we are "putting on Christ." This is *spiritual grit*. Now it's time to get ready for the battle.

The Belt of Truth

The first thing we must put on is truth because the devil is a liar. The truth of Jesus will defeat the lies of the evil one. Jesus said, "I am the way, the truth, and the life" (John 14:6).

He is the only way to God, the only one who can give eternal life, and He is the whole truth and nothing but the truth. Jesus is the only human being to see life as it really is. Only by having His understanding and perspective can we understand spiritual realities. The belt of truth or the truth of Jesus will help you in two ways: guidance and discernment.

Guidance. Amazing men need guidance; we always need to be going in the right direction. Therefore, it's important to listen to the right voice. The evil one always lies or twists the truth. The world makes false promises. The ego seeks fleeting pleasure or relief from pain. Jesus, through the Holy Spirit and His Word, will always tell you the truth and the good plans that He has for you. As you listen to His voice through your new heart, you'll always find your true north. You'll know what to love, what to hate, how to suffer well, and what to invest in and live for.

Discernment. Amazing men need discernment as well. The apostle John warns us,

> Beloved, don't believe every spirit, but test the spirits, whether they are of God, because many false prophets have gone out into the world. (1 John 4:1)

Even when you are pointed in the right direction, you'll still need discernment along the way. Life is a journey and there are many people and forces that will try to trip you up, especially in matters of religion. Do you know how to *test the spirits*?

Jonathan Edwards wrote a book entitled *The Distinguishing Marks of a Work of the Spirit of God*. In it, he gives five marks to know the truth.

1. Will Jesus be honored?
2. Will the devil and his kingdom be opposed?
3. Will the Word of God be highly regarded?
4. Will the truth of God be revealed?
5. Will God and others be loved?

A summary of the belt of truth is the Sermon on the Mount (Matthew 5–7).

The Chest-plate of Righteousness

The chest-plate covers your vital organs, where your deepest emotions come from. It is the area where joy, anger, fear, sadness, disgust, shame, and despair show up. We say things like "That makes me sick to my stomach" or "My heart is aching." Feelings are a big deal and need protection from evil. How does the righteousness of Christ protect us?

The righteousness of Christ protects us all the time, but especially when we fail. Let's say that you were having a bad day—I mean a *really* bad day. You walk in the door and someone you love, your wife or daughter, asks you for a favor. You answer harshly or you blow up. What if you stumble on to an evil internet site, you stretch the truth, someone cuts you off in traffic, or you find yourself desiring someone other than your spouse? Afterward you're sorry, but the damage is done.

> "Why did I do that?"
> "I'm never going to be free."
> "I'm sorry but I failed again."
> "I'm inadequate as a man."
> "God is angry and distant."

This is why you have the righteousness of Christ. Satan, the accuser, loves to make you feel inadequate, especially if you're counting on your own righteous behavior. In fact, he prefers that you think that way. He hates it when you count on Christ because he knows that Christ can resist and defeat him. When you count on the righteousness of Christ, then you know that all of your sins and failures have been forgiven: past, present, and future. You also know that your worth and value come from being loved by God. Not only are you forgiven, but you are also loved as a son. The God who made everything thought that you were worth dying for and is always glad to be with you. This righteousness is not what you do; it's who you are. We need this now more than ever.

Dr. Lewis Smedes wrote,

> Anyone who can see the needs of people today must recognize that the malaise of our time is an epidemic of self-doubt and self-depreciation. Those whose job it is to heal people's spiritual problems know that the overwhelming majority of people who seek help, are people who are sick from abhorring themselves. A prevailing sense of being without worth is the pervasive sickness of our age.

It is in the righteousness of Christ that you are deeply valued by God. And if God feels that way about you, then you should see yourself the same way.

This does not mean that God looks the other way on the things we know are wrong in our lives. He doesn't dismiss our sin. Instead, He deals with us as a Father, not as a mere judge but in love and patient discipline. In fact, I know I'm a son because of His discipline. My father once said to me, "John, I love you so much that I'm not going to let you get away with anything that will hurt you." I didn't understand it then, but I'm thankful for it now.

You can never lose the righteousness of Christ, and you will always be protected, even on your worst day. Say this in prayer:

> What I am is what Christ has made me. I'm not standing on my righteousness; I'm standing on His. When my Heavenly Father looks at me, He sees the perfect and active obedience of Jesus. I am accepted by grace, and my circumstances or failures do not make any difference at all.

That will keep your heart from discouragement and despair.

Brain science teaches us that the righteousness of Christ doesn't just protect our chest but the right side of our brain as well. He promises this: "I will in no way leave you, neither will I in any way forsake you" (Hebrews 13:5).

The Father and the Son enjoyed the most intimate and joyful relationship ever, and you and I are brought into that intimacy through the righteousness of Jesus. We are in "the Beloved" (Ephesians 1:6).

The Shoes of the Gospel of Peace

Shoes are essential to fighting and defeating the enemy. Imagine a soldier dressed in armor from head to ankle but with no shoes on. The rough ground would tear up his feet. If he were on an incline, he would lose his balance. Despite the fact that he had all of the other equipment, he would soon be on the sidelines. His feet would render him unfit to fight. But with the right shoes, he would be ready and able to fight. That is what this phrase means. The word for *shoes,* in this context from Ephesians 6, is actually translated *readiness.* "Your feet shod with the readiness produced by the good news of peace." It is peace in the heart that makes you ready and able to fight.

What does this mean? Once again it is Christ, but this time, it is Christ our peace, the source of our serenity. Notice the importance of the order of getting dressed. The first piece tells us that Christ is the truth, the ultimate secret of reality. The key to life and truth is Jesus Christ. He is something for the mind to understand and grasp and be connected to. Then what? We receive His righteousness. We rely on His perfect obedience. We put on the chest-plate of His righteousness. We come on the basis of what He has done and not our own performance. And what is the result of that? Our hearts are at peace! The apostle Paul says that because we have been justified by the righteousness of Christ, we have peace with God (Romans 5:1).

We have serenity and courage. Athletes speak of being in the zone where everything slows down. The peace of Christ puts us in the zone. We are ready for anything. No ground can be too rough for Christ. And we have Christ; therefore, we have optimism and hope.

Our battle is not a battle against people; it is an inner fight, a battle in the realm of the mind. It is a battle in the realm of your outlook upon the situation in which you find yourself. That's the place to start. Put on the belt of truth. In Jesus Christ, you have a powerful life that no man can equal, anywhere in the world. He is the key to life, the One who is worth listening to. Believe what He says. Act on it. Live your life based on Him. That is the belt of truth.

The chest-plate of righteousness protects the emotions. You do not have to live in fear and discouragement. Of course, you will fail at times, but you'll learn to overcome. Jesus understands all this. He knows we will fail, and He knows we will struggle. He knows it will be a roller-coaster experience, a time of battles, and that we will lose some of them. But He says,

> I have taken care of all that. You do not have to stand on your merits. You stand on mine. Do not be discouraged, do not be defeated, we will be victorious. I know what I am doing, I know how to lead you, I know what circumstances to bring you into, and I will bring you through them to victory.

The third piece of clothing is to have the shoes, the readiness of a sense of peace. The place to start is to remember who you are, what you are, and above all else, who you are joined to. Be strong in His strength and for His sake. This is your secret identity. Remember you belong to Christ's family. The scripture says He is not ashamed to call us brothers. God is not ashamed to be called our God. Be strong in the Lord!

In our next chapter, let's look at the rest of the armor.

Questions for Chapter 12

1. If the "belt of truth … will help you in two ways: guidance and discernment," in what areas of your life do you most need truth at this time? Will you ask God for the wisdom that He promises He will give you?

2. The text says that "feelings are a big deal and they need protection from evil." How has the chest-plate of righteousness protected you in the past? How do you need that protection right now?

3. Dr. Smedes wrote, "The malaise of our time is an epidemic of self-doubt and self-depreciation." Do you ever feel that way, and how might the spiritual armor help you with that?

4. Are you encouraged when you read, "When my Heavenly Father looks at me, He sees the perfect and active obedience of Jesus. I am accepted by grace, and my circumstances or failures do not make any difference at all"? How has knowing that helped you recently?

5. In the section about the Gospel of peace, peace is expressed as serenity, courage, optimism and hope, being in the zone, ready for anything. If you lack any of these things, what could you do to get them?

Chapter 13

SPIRITUAL ARMOR: PART 2

The Shield of Faith

Let's take a closer look at the battle we're in. If we remind ourselves that Christ is the source of truth, that Christ is our righteousness, and that Christ is our peace, our hearts should be at rest. But there are times when these reminders are not enough. We are still depressed. We are still filled with doubts, still disturbed. What is happening? We are experiencing what Paul calls "the fiery darts of the evil one."

These are part of the schemes of the devil, the strategies of Satan. They come to us in various forms. Sometimes they are evil thoughts and ideas that burst in suddenly on our thinking in the most unlikely moments. We may be reading the Bible, focused in prayer, or driving to work when, all of a sudden, some dark or lustful thought flashes into our mind. What is that? One of the fiery darts of the evil one! We have to recognize it. And while Satan cannot read your mind, he can put thoughts in your mind. God is omniscient. He knows our every thought. Satan does not.

In whatever form they may come to us, they always have two characteristics. First, they seem to arise out of our own thoughts. They seem to come right from inside of us. We say to ourselves, "This is something I am thinking."

Oftentimes it is a shocking thing. But the devil is really communicating to us. He is trying to influence us, even though it doesn't seem like that to us.

Secondly, they are always an attack upon our position in Christ as the truth, our righteousness, and our peace. These darts are always meant to raise doubts about our position in Christ. The devil asked Eve in the garden, "Did God really say that?" (Genesis 3:1).

There is the innuendo of doubt. He said to Jesus, "If you are the Son of God, command that these stones become bread" (Matthew 4:3, Luke 4:3).

That word *if!* There is always the suggestion that these things are not true. This is the way he raises doubts, creates guilt, and triggers fear.

How are we to combat these things successfully? Paul says by taking up the shield of faith (Ephesians 6:16). What does that mean?

Faith is acting upon belief. Faith is a decision, resolution, and action. Faith is saying, "Yes, I believe Christ is the truth. He is my righteousness; He is my peace. Therefore, this thought must be a lie."

Faith is working out the implications of belief. When you say, "Therefore," you move from belief into faith. Faith is taking hold of what you believe. It is taking the general truth, applying it to your specific situation, and saying, "If this is true, then this must follow." That is the shield of faith. Have you learned how to take the shield of faith when doubts come? Here's how to respond:

> Christ is the truth. He is the revelation of things that really are. He has demonstrated it. Therefore, I cannot accept this thought that Christianity is a hoax. I cannot believe both. I cannot believe that Christ is the truth and that this thing I'm tempted to believe is true also. I have committed myself to Christ because I have been persuaded that He has completely demonstrated truth. I stand on that ground. Therefore, I must reject this lie.

You can also say,

> Christ is my righteousness. I am linked with Him. I am one with Him. His life is my life, and my life is His life. I am

inseparably joined to Him. Therefore, I cannot believe this lie that these evil thoughts are my thoughts. They are not my thoughts at all. They are thoughts that come into my mind from the evil one. It is not my thinking at all. No, it is the devil again. I do not want these thoughts. I will not listen to them. I reject them. I do not want them in my thinking. They are from the devil's minions and I'll send them back where they belong!

Using the shield of faith means refusal to feel condemned or to feel guilty without any hope. Christ is the basis of my peace. Therefore, it is his responsibility to take me through everything. He is the Adequate One. He has come to see me through every situation. So I will not believe this fear, this sudden anxiety that grips my heart. I will not believe that it is from me. It is simply sent to shake my confidence in Christ. It is an attempt to destroy my peace. But Christ is adequate for even this and therefore I refuse to be intimidated by it.

James says to resist the devil and he will flee from you (James 4:7).

He will flee from you. You do it again and again every time the thought comes back; you resist it on that basis. You refuse to give up your position in Christ. Inevitably, the doubts will clear. Your feelings will change, the attacks will cease, and you will be back again experiencing the love and joy of God. That is what Paul is talking about.

The shield of faith is enough in itself. It is all you need.

However, there are two more pieces of armor. The last two pieces of armor are given so that we might be more than conquerors (Romans 8:37).

We are not only going to win, we are going to win triumphantly and abundantly. The apostle John said that the one who lives inside us is greater than the devil, who is in the world (1 John 4:4).

The apostle Paul adds that when sin multiplies, there is more grace to defeat it (Romans 5:20).

We are intended to do more than barely squeak by in life. We are designed to triumph, to be fearless, to be unconquerable, to have spiritual grit, and to be amazing. For that, we need a helmet and a sword!

The Helmet of Salvation

The figure of a helmet suggests that this is designed to protect the mind: the ability to think clearly. The helmet can keep our thinking straight and preserve us from mental confusion and darkness when the world around us seems out of control.

In 2020, we faced a pandemic called COVID 19—765 million cases and nearly 7 million deaths. The worldwide lockdown affected businesses and people's livelihoods. Fortunes were ruined. Our world and especially our country, are deeply divided politically and socially. There have been protests (violent and peaceful), looting, destruction of property, and killings. We have narcissistic leaders on both sides of the aisle in Washington and running state governments, fighting for power and control. Doctors and psychologists have dubbed the state we're in as *crisis fatigue*. Others say we're in a "new normal," whatever that is. Today more than ever we need the helmet of salvation.

There is no protection in the world for the mind, but the Christian has the helmet of salvation. Paul is not looking back at all. He is not speaking of salvation as a past decision that we made when we were justified. When that happened, we put on truth, righteousness, and peace. He also is not talking about a present experience or sanctification. He is looking to the future. He is talking about a salvation that will be a future event. Listen to what he says in another passage:

> But since we belong to the day, let's be sober, putting on the breastplate of faith and love, and for a helmet, the hope of salvation. (1 Thessalonians 5:8)

In this verse, salvation is a hope, something yet in the future, something not yet possessed or fully enjoyed. This future tense of salvation is described for us in a number of passages, but very plainly and fully in Romans 8:18–25 and especially in verses 22–25.

In these verses, Paul is talks about the day of resurrection, the day of the coming again of Christ, the day when creation will be delivered from its bondage, the day when Christ returns to establish His kingdom. This helmet, therefore, is the recognition that all human schemes to obtain world peace and harmony are doomed to fail. But through these failures, Jesus Christ is working out His own plan that will culminate in his appearing again and the establishment of His own reign in righteousness on the earth. This is the helmet of salvation that will keep your thinking straight in the hour of man's confusion and darkness.

We are not to be taken in by the unreal and groundless utopian expectations of the world, nor are we to withdraw from the world and isolate ourselves. We are to be involved in what is going on in the world for a wholly different reason than others. *We are to be involved in order to accomplish God's desire to confront men everywhere, at every level, in all enterprises of life, with the good news of God's salvation in Jesus Christ.*

There are also many causes that we can join. There are aims that we can wholeheartedly endorse. We are always to be humanitarian—helping the weak, ministering to the sick, and helping those who are old, in prison, or burdened in some way. We should always be ready to further good government, because government is of God. Christians ought to be ready to alleviate social evil and to further understanding between countries if given the chance. Read the injunctions of scripture.

- The powers that be are ordained of God (Romans 13:1).
- Honor all men (1 Peter 2:17).
- Do good to all (1 Peter 3:11).
- Honor the king (1 Peter 2:17).

- Obey your masters (Colossians 3:22).
- Provide things honest before all men (Romans 12:17).
- Feed the hungry, clothe the naked, heal the sick (Matthew 10:8, Luke 10:9).

These are practical exhortations. Look at the life of the Lord Jesus Himself. Here's how Peter summed up His life:

> Jesus of Nazareth ... who went about doing good and healing all who were oppressed by the devil, for God was with him. (Acts 10:38)

Our labor is not in vain. That gives us grit—spiritual grit. Now let's discuss the last piece of armor.

The Sword of the Spirit

The apostle Paul tells us what this piece of armor is: the Word of God. There are two Greek words used for scripture, *logos* and *rhema*. *Logos* refers to the complete revelation of what God has said. *Rhema* means a specific saying of God, a passage or a verse that has special application to an immediate situation; it is the Word of God applied to our current experience, to our existence. This is a great spiritual weapon, especially when placed in the hands of an amazing man.

The sword is the only offensive weapon mentioned, but it was also used for defense, when an enemy came in close for combat. We are not to fight the enemy with our own ideas or strength but with the Word of God, properly understood and applied.

Satan uses three tactics.

1. He will try to get you to prioritize your physical life over your spiritual life. It might be food, sex, wealth, power, or even your looks. What was Jesus doing when Satan showed up?

He was fasting and communing with His Father. Fasting is useful for sharpening our focus on God. Satan wanted to break up Jesus's communion. He wanted Jesus to prioritize His desire for food.

2. He will attempt to get you to put your will and wishes above God's will. This is the sin of presumption. He'll even give you scripture taken out of context. You must see through the smokescreen and use your sword.

3. He will tempt you to make a lesser pursuit of yours into the most important thing in life, a kind of worship. This may often be found in the pages of a self-help book or a motivational speaker. It could even be a good thing. You might attain or possess it, but it will consume your life.

The instructive thing for us is that each time, Jesus responded with a specific, appropriate scripture that He knew verbatim from memory. He knew the Word and used it to ward off Satan's temptations. We should do the same.

Defensive Use of the Sword

We must use the sword (scripture) to fight off the temptations and attacks of the enemy.

As we said, Jesus is our example. He used God's Word defensively against the devil when he tempted Him in Matthew 4. Jesus hadn't eaten in forty days, so the devil suggested, "If you're the Son of God, turn these stones into bread."

Jesus answered by quoting Deuteronomy 8:3. "Man shall not live by bread alone, but by every word that proceeds out of God's mouth" (Matthew 4:4).

Jesus gave priority to the spiritual over the physical and rejected the devil's advice.

Next, Satan took Jesus up to the pinnacle of the temple and

suggested that He throw Himself down. Satan himself quoted from Psalm 91:11–12.

> For He will put his angels in charge of you, *to guard you in all your ways.* They will bear you up in their hands, so that you won't dash your foot against a stone.

The devil left out the phrase "to guard you in all your ways." Satan knows scripture and can twist it to tempt you. Be on your guard! Jesus rebutted the devil with Deuteronomy 6:16.

> Again, it is written, "you shall not test the Lord your God."

Satan wasn't finished. He took Jesus to a high mountain and showed Him all the kingdoms of the world and their glory. Then he said,

> I will give you all of these things, if you fall down and worship me. (Matthew 4:9)

Jesus again came back quoting scripture from Deuteronomy 6:13.

> Get behind me, Satan! For it is written, you shall worship the Lord your God, and you shall serve Him only.

Offensive Use of the Sword

You don't need to be under attack to use the sword. You can use it in all of your relationships and use it in many situations and opportunities. You don't have to say, "The Bible says …" or even give the reference. It doesn't lose any of its power.

I use scripture when I to talk to people, especially my friends and family. I'm not a Bible thumper, but I drop it in when appropriate. It not only protects me but also pierces the hearts of others and can expose the lies of the devil for them. This is its great effect. I especially use it when I am counseling or giving guidance. I always use it when I teach in any setting, even if it's subtle. I even use it when I'm talking to unbelievers so that their eyes might be opened. It's amazing how the right word at the right time can open the eyes of the blind.

> For the word of God is living and active and sharper than any two-edged sword, piercing even to dividing of soul and spirit, of both joints and marrow and is able to discern the thoughts and intentions of the heart. (Hebrews 4:12)

Read it, listen to it, study it, memorize it, then use it, and you will be victorious!

Questions for Chapter 13

1. How can the *shield of faith* help us deal with the times when evil thoughts come at us unexpectedly from Satan?

2. What is your response to reading the following: "Using the shield of faith means refusal to feel condemned or to feel guilty without any hope. Christ is the basis of my peace. Therefore, it is His responsibility to take me through everything"?

3. How can the *helmet of salvation* protect our minds and our ability to think clearly and help us to face the future with joy and without fear? How have you experienced this in your life? In what ways do you need to use the helmet more effectively?

4. Since Jesus "went about doing good" and our labor is not in vain, what could you do on a practical level to do good unto others and make this a better world? To what causes is your heart attuned to, and in what ways are you uniquely gifted to contribute?

5. This chapter says that the *sword of the Spirit* can be used defensively. What examples can you think of for how you could do this when you are tempted to sin?

6. How might you use the *sword* offensively when you are talking to others about the Lord?

7. Are you digging into the Word of God regularly so that it will readily come to mind as you need it? If not, what will it take for you to be more faithful in your devotional life?

Chapter 14

SPIRITUAL ARMOR: PART 3

Overcoming the Ego (Our Old Nature)

Have you ever considered doing something that you knew was wrong and went ahead and did it anyway? Or have you ever been impressed to do something good but you neglected to do it? Then afterward you vowed to never act that way again, but you did anyway! Paul expresses it this way:

> For the good which I desire, I don't do; but the evil which I don't desire, that I practice. (Romans 7:19)

Why do we experience that? Here's why:

> For the flesh (ego) lusts against the Spirit, and the Spirit against the flesh (ego), for these are contrary to one another, that you may not do the things that you desire. (Galatians 5:17)

You have two sets of desires inside of you. One set comes from the ego, and the other set comes from the Spirit.

Where did these two sets of desires come from?

- You were *born* with the desires from the ego.
- You were *born again* with the desires of the Spirit.

What is the flesh? It gets confusing because we automatically think of flesh along physical lines, but that is not what Paul is referring to here. It's also called the *old nature* or *ego.* Whenever I see the word *nature* used in a spiritual sense, I think of *disposition.* The ego is a hostile disposition toward God. It came into being when Adam and Eve sinned in Genesis 3. Here is a definition:

> The flesh is the ego that feels a deep emptiness inside and uses the resources in its own power to try to fill it. Ego is the "I" who tries to satisfy me with anything other than God's mercy and grace.

Before you came to Christ, your ego was in charge. It had a master-slave relationship with you. You may have even defined yourself by it. For some people, the ego is expressed in rebellion. For others, it is expressed in moralism. For still others, it's expressed in religion. No matter, it is the proud ego that says, "I did it my way!"

What about the other set of desires? They come from the Spirit of God. When you came to Christ, the Spirit put to death the dominating power of the old nature and gave you a new nature or a new disposition with a desire to please God and submit to His rule.

You may be asking, "If I have a new nature that desires to please God, then why do I have this internal struggle?" It is because the new nature on its own doesn't have the power to defeat the old nature. The old nature can still defeat the new nature on its own every time.

When the old nature was put to death, it was put to death in its position as master. It still has influence, but it is no longer in charge. We have a new master—Jesus—and the Spirit is applying the life of Jesus to our new nature. Only the Holy Spirit can provide the power to overcome the ego as we "walk by the Spirit."

> But I say, walk by the Spirit, and you won't fulfill the lust of the flesh. (Galatians 5:16)

So how do we walk in the Spirit?

> But if you are led by the Spirit, you are not under the law.
> (Galatians 5:18)

Being led by the Spirit and walking in the Spirit are the same thing. What does it mean to be led? It means to be continually connected to the Spirit. The more you are led, the more the struggle eases. It's like being hooked up to a powerful diesel engine pulling a trailer. The ego will always present a desire to slow you down or disconnect you, but the Spirit will give you the power to overcome it. At the moment of temptation, recognize the Spirit's presence in your life and ask for His help. Even if you don't know what to ask for, the Spirit does.

> In the same way the Spirit also helps our weaknesses, for we don't know how to pray as we ought, but the Spirit himself makes intercession for us with groanings which can't be uttered. (Romans 8:26)

Make it your aim to form a deep bond of love with the Father, the Son, and the Holy Spirit. Ask the Spirit to put to death the deeds of the ego. Make an inventory of the areas of your life and give the Holy Spirit control of them all. I recently confessed some sins of my youth and asked the Holy Spirit to take away the memories. He put them to death.

> For if you live after the flesh, you must die; but if by the Spirit you put to death the deeds of the body, you will live. (Romans 8:13)

> But the fruit of the Spirit is love, joy, peace, patience, kindness, goodness, faith, gentleness, and self-control. Against such things there is no law. (Galatians 5:22–23)

The evidence that you are walking in the Spirit is clear: the fruit of the Spirit will begin to define your life. Did you know that all of these qualities are manifestations of the first one, love? Joy is love enjoying itself, peace is love resting, patience is love waiting, kindness is love reacting, goodness is love initiating, faithfulness is love keeping its word, gentleness is love validating, and self-control is love resisting temptation. Love is the key; love is the main thing. When you love God and love others, and even love your enemies, you are walking in the Spirit.

The only way the Spirit can produce this love in you is to help you abide in Christ. Walking in the Spirit is the same as abiding in Christ (John 15).

How do you know you're abiding? You are abiding when you are resting in the promises of God. How do you know you're resting? When you're resting, only Jesus can satisfy your soul. We stand on the promises of God!

How is all this applied? By faith.

> I have been crucified with Christ, and it is no longer I who live, but Christ lives in me. That life which I now live in the flesh, I live by faith in the Son of God, who loved me, and gave himself up for me. (Galatians 2:20)

We were not originally designed with an old nature. We deal with our old nature on a daily basis by being led by God's Spirit. We were supposed to be like Jesus, who didn't have an old nature (John 14:30).

The world system, as organized by fallen rebels, can be both attractive and seductive. Satan is also clever and subtle, a dangerous enemy. But the ego is a man's worst enemy. The ego provides internal access for the devil and the world to destroy you. You have a traitor inside, and this enemy is relentless. When we are not victorious over the world and the devil, it is because we are being defeated on the ground of our old, independent self. The indwelling Holy Spirit seeks to free us from that traitor.

A World War II chaplain stationed in the South Pacific said,

The greatest enemy we face aboard our ships is not the Japanese planes or subs, but rust. Today we scrape, tomorrow we paint, so the next day we can paint again.

He went on to say that though the enemies of battle rested from their attacks on certain days, the vicious enemy of rust never rested. We have found that to be true with ourselves. The ego is like rust. There are days when the world holds no attraction for us and the devil has fled, but there is never a day that we are not troubled with our ego that wants to rule.

The new nature that we receive when we become a new creation in Christ can never defeat the old nature on its own. We must be empowered by the Holy Spirit. Only the Holy Spirit has the power to overcome the old nature in this internal conflict. How do we draw on this power?

But I say, walk by the Spirit, and you won't fulfill the lust (desires) of the flesh. For the flesh lusts against the Spirit, and the Spirit against the flesh; for these are contrary to one another, that you may not do the things that you desire. (Galatians 5:16–17)

If we live by the Spirit, let's also walk by (keep in step with) the Spirit. (Galatians 5:25)

Paul says the secret to spiritual grit is to "walk by the Spirit." Don't do any walking (living) without the Spirit.

Questions for Chapter 14

1. What are the typical "desires of the ego" that gnaw at you most frequently?
2. Do you regularly experience overcoming your ego's desires by relying on the Holy Spirit? If not, how might you grow spiritually in this area?
3. What does it mean to you to be "led by the Spirit"?
4. In your life, are you experiencing an increase of the fruit of the Spirit? Which of them are strengths for you and which are weaknesses: love, joy, peace, patience, kindness, goodness, faithfulness, gentleness, and self-control?
5. What does it mean to walk by or keep in step with the Spirit? How might you do better at that?

Chapter 15

A GENTLE PROTECTOR: HOW A MAN LEADS OTHERS

We noted earlier that God has hardwired our brains to detect weakness in others. Why would He do that? He did it so that we could protect others, cultivate them, and give them a group identity through trust, joy, and relational engagement. Our strength is given to help people thrive and flourish.

Not all men use their strength well. According to Jim Wilder, there are three types of men in the world: *predators, possums,* and *gentle protectors.* Predators pounce on weakness, possums hide their weakness, and gentle protectors are tender toward weakness. Our strength must be tamed. To become a gentle protector takes a measure of maturity and a lot of practice.

What We Need to Practice

Gentle protectors practice five habits. They

- lead from a strong and brave heart
- create hospitality
- receive and give life
- recover from trauma
- amplify potential

Leading from a Strong and Brave Heart

The heart we are talking about is not the muscular organ that pumps blood to your body. The heart we are talking about refers to

- spiritual discernment—life in the power of the Spirit
- true identity and destiny (Moses didn't have a healthy heart till he was eighty.)

We were born with weak and deceptive hearts.

- Weak means a false understanding of good and evil.
- Deceptive means a fatal tendency to convince myself and others that I am right.

But God gives us a new heart! (Ezekiel 36:25–28)

We must learn to love and lead out of this new heart. As we learn, we practice. As we practice, we grow.

Paul's prayer in Ephesians 1:18–19 is that we would know the following three things:

1. the hope to which God has called us
2. the riches of His glorious inheritance in us
3. the immeasurable greatness of God's power available to us

This knowledge comes from "having the eyes of our new heart enlightened." How do we have our new hearts enlightened even more?

Where our eyes look determines what we see. When the spiritual eyes of our heart are turned toward God, we see truth and receive guidance and discernment. We begin to consciously experience our calling, our inheritance, and God's power. New hearts react in new ways: we are strong and brave.

Characteristics of New Hearts

1. Our hearts were designed for joy and relationships.
   At nine months, a baby and mother can spend up to eight hours a day looking at one another.

   In the same way, we are motivated by love to focus our spiritual eyes on God. He is our treasure. He brings us joy. Not only that, but I understand He wants to be with me. I see that relationships matter to God (the Trinity itself is a community). I begin to move into relationships that reflect my relationship with God. I see people the way God sees them, the way they were meant to be. I become an ambassador of joy.

2. Our hearts were designed to handle the stress of
   - anger
   - fear
   - sadness
   - disgust
   - shame
   - overwhelming despair

   I can experience these powerful emotions and still return to *joy!*

3. Our hearts were designed to serve.
   To experience significance in life, you must serve with others in ministry. Ministry just means doing good to other people.

   Significance does not come from status, a hood ornament on your car, or a logo on your shirt. Significance does not come from a bigger salary. Significance does not come from sex. Significance comes from service. Significance comes when you think about other people's needs as well as your own. You cannot be selfish and significant at the same time.

> As each has received a gift, employ it in serving one another, as good managers of the grace of God in its various forms. (1 Peter 4:10)

4. Our hearts were designed to create hospitality. You can create hospitality everywhere you go.
5. Our hearts were designed to recover, to be panic proof, and to suffer well. It is the people of God that God uses to transform suffering.
6. Our hearts were designed to function best in community. This is why we need deep relationships.

We must learn to know our hearts in order to fully thrive. We can have either a healthy heart or an unhealthy one. A healthy heart is alive and full of the presence of Jesus. Through this gift, we become the person that we were designed to be. An unhealthy heart is one that serves the ego and is always operating out of hurt. The ego is your old heart—your natural disposition. It is the organ of deceptive knowing—the fallen human nature. Through a new heart that is strong and brave, we see and hear in our spirit. When we love God with all our heart, we stay synchronized with Him. Synching up with God keeps our hearts strong.

Creating Hospitality

Creating secure attachment with others is hospitality. In the New Testament, hospitality seems to be less of a specific activity (such as inviting someone to your home for dinner) and more of a mindset of letting strangers into your life. Hospitality is not an event and doesn't require a certain space. It can be shown anywhere.

Creating hospitality is creating a safe space for others, including them, and treating them as people made in the image of God, which is what they are. More and more, our world is becoming relationally dysfunctional. We don't care about the clerk who checks us out at the grocery store; we only care that they're fast and efficient. The medical world seems to be getting worse in its bedside manner. We are becoming impersonal. We miss all kinds of relational moments because we're self-focused and in a hurry.

Recently in Florida, I was at a checkout and only two registers were open. Needless to say, both lines were long. I was behind a lady whose grocery cart was filled and overflowing. I had just a couple of items. Patience is one of the fruits of the Spirit that still needs lots of development in me, so I surrendered to the life lesson. When the woman reached the front, she turned to me and said, "Would you like to go ahead of me?" I was stunned. I almost fell to my knees in prayer and thanksgiving. In that moment, that wonderful woman practiced hospitality toward me. I would not be surprised to learn that she knows God. She certainly lives with a strong heart!

Creating hospitality is all throughout the Bible, including the following scriptures:

- the Garden of Eden (Genesis 2)
- the cultural mandate (Genesis 1:26–28; 2:15)
- Abraham and the Canaanite kings (Genesis 14)
- Joseph in Egypt (Genesis 39–50)
- Jesus created hospitality and secure attachments all throughout His life with all kinds of people: prostitutes, tax collectors, the broken, the outcasts, businessmen, and the religious. He told the disciples, "Don't let your heart to be troubled." (John 14:1)

This is the work of God and the work of the kingdom of God.

Amazing men will be known by their ability to create hospitality and secure attachments.

Having a family and community to belong to is essential for a person to

- have a foundation
- have a place for growth
- have an identity
- reach one's God-given potential
- form joy attachments

The family of God includes many people who God brings into your life to give you what your heart needs. We all need to belong and learn to create hospitality and secure attachment for others.

Receiving and Giving Life

Jesus said that anyone who believes in Him will have rivers of living water flowing within them. These rivers are a metaphor for the life of the Spirit within us. This makes us a life-giving force in the world.

The Sea of Galilee

The Sea of Galilee is found in northern Israel. In Jesus's time, the area around the water was a string of thriving cities because the sea was teeming with life! The fisheries of this region were famous throughout the Roman Empire and provided a robust trade. This was the sea where Jesus found His "fishers of men." It's the same sea where Jesus told the disciples to cast their nets on the other side of their boat. They caught so many fish that they struggled to bring them all in.

The Dead Sea

The sea to the south is called the Dead Sea, and for good reason. Some believe ancient earthquakes exposed the sea to an unusually high amount of chemicals that are incompatible with aquatic life. It may have been caused by the curse on Sodom. Twenty-five percent of the water is made up of salt, bromide, and similar chemicals that make life impossible.

Geographically, these two bodies of water are only sixty-three miles apart. How is it that one teems with life while the other is famous for death?

If you look closely at a map, you'll notice one distinct difference. The northern Sea of Galilee is fed from the north and in turn feeds the famous Jordan River to the south. Water comes in, and water goes out.

However, the southern sea is in "receive only" mode. All water flows in, but none flows out. Even the tributaries seen to the east of the Dead Sea feed *into* the Dead Sea. One sea is full of life and the other sea is full of death.

In our first four years of life, the main task that we have to accomplish is learning to receive life through joyful relationships. We should learn that we matter and that people (family) love to be with us no matter how we feel or what we're going through. Our parents delight in us and build love/life bonds with us. We learn to live in joy, to expand our capacity for joy, and to build *joy strength*. We develop trust and we organize our personality through relationships. We learn that joy is our natural state and we learn to return to joy through relationships.

While the rest of our development involves learning to give life and joy to others, we first learn to take care of our own needs. Slowly we learn to give life to another, then another, then a group. We bring life and joy to the people around us.

Sadly, some people never learned to receive because they were never valued for their unique identity. They develop a weak identity dominated by fear and coldness or by people-pleasing tendencies. Because they never learned to receive, it's hard for them to give life and joy. They experience frustration and disappointment. They can become passive-aggressive and develop addictions as a replacement for the joy of being with people who enjoy being with them. They are also prone to repeating familial dysfunction and lies. The worst thing that happens to them is they are *stuck* in destructive patterns!

Death is the absence of life. Death is emptiness, loneliness, misery, depression, boredom, and restlessness. Some people never seem to have anything but death in their lives.

A leader who learns to thrive is one who has learned to receive. Even if he/she didn't receive love bonds as a child, our "Abba Father" loves and values our unique identity. After all, He designed us just as we are. Jesus loves us so much that He gave His life for us. We receive His life. The first Adam brought death, but the last Adam (Jesus Christ) is a life-giving Spirit. When we are born from above, we get to start life over and develop the way we were supposed to. We have this life force living inside of us.

What is life? It is more than physical existence. Life is love, joy, and excitement. It is vitality, enrichment, power; it is fulfillment in every direction, in every possibility of your being. That is life.

Christ's death provides such abundant grace and loving acceptance, which are available again and again, so that all who are in Him can reign in life now. You can have life in the midst of all the pressures, circumstances, suffering, and troubles. Your spirit can be alive and joyful—experiencing fulfillment and delight. Life in the midst of death! Someday we will rule over the angels, but we must learn to reign in life now. Love, joy, peace, glory, and gladness fill our hearts even in the midst of all the heartaches and pressures of life. Then we become a channel of life for others!

Redemption from Trauma

Everyone suffers. For some, the suffering traumatizes them. Others learn to *suffer well*. We discussed Joseph earlier when we talked of emotional quotient. As a young man, he was traumatized. Here's the background from Genesis 37:

Joseph's family was extremely dysfunctional: multiple moms with eleven boys and then Joseph—Jacob's favorite son. Jacob made no secret of his bias, and Joseph was sometimes naïve and somewhat proud. His brothers hated him and planned to kill him. These sons were vengeful and picked up the family dysfunction.

Despite the dysfunctional nature of the family, Joseph learned to receive and give life. He was given various tasks and responsibilities. He learned to take care of himself and was learning to take care of others. Still, his brothers despised him, and when the opportunity came, they sold him into slavery. Being sold into slavery could have traumatized him, but it didn't. Instead, he suffered well. He had the emotional capacity to handle the trauma. Over the next twenty years, God maximized his maturity so that he could take care of a nation (Egypt) and ultimately restore his family.

Emotional capacity refers to the amount of stress you can handle before things blow up or melt down. When your emotional capacity gets overwhelmed, trauma occurs and your ability to suffer well gets stunted. Trauma stunts the development of capacity.

How we receive and give life on earth is subject to the ravages of trauma. Most of us have been affected by trauma, resulting in the desynchronization of our minds and relationships. We no longer receive when it is time to receive or give when it is time to give. Whether it was something bad that happened (type B trauma) or an absence of a necessary, good thing (type A trauma), we all need recovery.

We have achieved *redemption and recovery* when we exceed our current capacity and reach our God-intended destiny. The devastating results of trauma can lead to desynchronization with other people and within our own brain. Scripture calls this a "divided heart." We cannot live to our potential when our brain is not synchronized with itself and others. The devastating results of trauma create a need to face and embrace past wounds, achieve resolution from trauma, and restore synchronization within our own mind and with others. This restoration is the work of God.

Many of the issues leaders face are directly related to their lack of emotional capacity, which failed to develop because of unresolved trauma. When this happens, it is easy to get stuck in our development so that we do not live with the level of maturity our position of responsibility and stage of life requires.

The apostle Paul didn't just lead people to Christ. He built a spiritual family; he was a father with many sons. He built relationships with these sons and mentored them as their spiritual father. Paul sent Timothy to the Corinthians as a model of maturity for them to emulate. Timothy, in turn, would help them build a multigenerational community in which the weak and the strong lived together.

Amplifying Potential

What prevents most people from reaching their full potential?

One author writes,

> The most common trap is fear. I've never met a 20-year-old or a 50-year-old who says, "I've never had a single passion, dream, hope, or desire." We all have them, but a lot of us give in to fear as soon as we get close to them. The reason is that fear only gets loud when you do things that matter. Fear never bothers you if you're average but the second you dare to be more than ordinary, fear awakens. (Jon Acuff)

What does it mean to amplify our potential?

It means to reach full maturity, to grow up!

When you think about life in any form, life is equal to growth. Growth is evidence of life. You plant a seed in the ground and it grows to a full-sized plant. That's the nature of life. You have a small puppy in your home and it grows to be a big dog. You have a baby in your home and it grows to be an adult. And that's the way life works. Life essentially can be defined as the dynamic of development or the dynamic of growth. Life is equal to growth. Where there's life, there's growth; where there's growth, there's life.

Physical Realm

With proper nurturing, nutrition, and exercise, we grow through stages: infants, children, young adults, parents, and elders.

Spiritual Realm

God intends for us to grow into spiritual maturity as well: to become adults, fathers, and elders. The goal of spiritual development is to become like Christ. It is also called

- following after righteousness
- being transformed by the renewing of your mind
- perfecting holiness in the fear of God
- pressing toward the mark
- being built up in the faith

Infancy and Childhood in the Spiritual Life

Here is the wonder of spiritual babes and children: God is my Father. Christ is my Savior! He protects me, He cares for me, He meets my needs, and He's preparing a place for me.

There is a delight in their spiritual life, delight in their spiritual experiences. It's not about information. It's not about theology. It's about relationship. Spiritual babies are attached to the relationship more than to doctrine.

Young Men/Adults

They have learned to overcome the evil one!

Fathers

They know God deeply.

Psychological/Personality Development

- Infants: I learn to receive.
- Children: I learn who I am and how to do hard stuff.
- Young adult: I learn fairness and how to take care of someone else simultaneously.
- Parent: I learn how to take care of others sacrificially (children).
- Elder: I learn how to take care of the community, especially the weak.

The following can block our maturity:

- unfinished trauma recovery
- the lack of life-giving relationships

What steps can help us reach our potential?

- Identify our spiritual and psychological age, which we don't identify by information or activities.
- Be with people who have a genuine desire to be with us and can show us how to have joy in the midst of negative feelings; building new bonds of love.
- Have the courage to pursue maturity.

- Get into a group that can help form our identity in Christ.
- Ask God for wisdom.

If you have failed to reach your potential at any stage, it's because you have been operating in fear. Remember our brains only run on one of two things: fear or joy. Let's choose joy.

When we belong, receive and give life, and recover from things that have gone wrong, the result is a growing level of maturity. The goal of maturity is to act out of a healthy heart—remaining our best self in all circumstances and situations. Maturity is about reaching one's God-given potential, maximizing skills and talents, and using them effectively while growing into the full capability of our individual designs. Our identities change along with our capacities as we transition through each stage of maturity. Belonging, receiving and giving life, and synchronizing improve as we mature. And we become amazing leaders and gentle protectors!

Questions for Chapter 15

1. This chapter begins by saying that God hardwires our brains to detect weakness in others. What are the reasons it gives for this?

2. It also states, *"Predators* pounce on weakness, *possums* hide their weakness, and *gentle protectors* are tender toward weakness." Other than when you are playing competitive sports, what is your most common response to weakness?

3. Do you desire to be a gentle protector? What would that look like in your life and with the relationships you currently have?

4. The five habits of a gentle protector are leading from a strong and brave heart, creating hospitality, receiving and giving life, recovering from trauma, and amplifying potential. Which of these are strengths for you and which are weaknesses? What might you do to become amazing in them all?

5. Our "new heart refers to spiritual discernment, true identity and destiny," which sometimes takes a long time to realize. If you have come to the point of knowing your identity and destiny, how would you describe them to another person?

6. "Our new heart was designed: for joy and relationship, to handle the stress, to serve others, to create hospitality, to recover and be panic proof, to suffer well, and to function best in community." Which of these areas would you want to work on becoming amazing?

7. What was the most important thing you learned from this long chapter? How will you incorporate it into your life?

Chapter 16

"Be Magnetic": How a Man Treats Others

How a Man Treats Women, Especially His Wife

A magnetic lover is a man who loves and leads his wife, who continually seeks to understand her and helps her sort things out, who practices the three kinds of love appropriately with her, who makes her safe and secure, who romances her for a lifetime, and who brings out the best in her. His magnetism grows so that he and his wife become one in body, soul, and spirit, reflecting the Trinity and the love of Christ.

One of the most difficult commands in scripture is found in 1 Peter 3:7. "Live with your wife in an understanding way." Women are not simple; they're complicated. They are mysterious, and God made them that way to bring out the best in men.

Here are eleven quick guidelines:

1. Love her unconditionally, mutually, and sexually.
2. Lead by example.
3. Never stop trying to understand her.
4. Romance her for a lifetime.
5. Bring out the best in her.
6. When you understand her, you make the changes that she needs you to make.
7. Bring your "A" game to the relationship.

8. Tithe to your wife with time—at least 10 percent.
9. Remember she is a girl, even if she's a tomboy.
10. Don't be ignorant, unskilled, or resentful!
11. Become one with her in every way.

❖ What does it mean to lead in the home?

As we said earlier, the apostle Peter identified the primary role of the husband in marriage: knowledgeable leadership. This emphasizes the responsibility of the husband in providing understanding leadership in his home. Every man is ultimately responsible to God for what his home becomes. This is what the scripture consistently teaches.

In writing to the Corinthians, Paul says,

> The Holy Spirit, through Paul, puts the responsibility of the husband to exercise knowledgeable leadership in the home within the framework of total leadership in the universe. (1 Corinthians 11:3)

Men must take this responsibility seriously. This is built into a man's nature, by divine mandate. There is not only a responsibility but also a desire to do this (inside the home, not outside of it).

A woman was made for this role in marriage and most women feel it even if they won't admit it. That flies in the face of political correctness, but the Bible often does. The problem is usually not so much due to the wife seeking to be the leader, as it is the refusal of the husband to assume his responsibility of leadership. Men fail by being indecisive and uncooperative.

In our American life, we don't emphasize teaching boys how to be men. Many men grow up and get married but are nothing more than little boys in grown-up bodies still looking for mothers rather than wives. They want someone to serve their physical needs, keep them well fed and happy, and soothe their egos when they get hurt.

They want someone to wait on them, to be there to fulfill whatever demand they may make. Recently Linda and I watched the movie *Uncle Buck,* starring John Candy (who I really miss as an actor). In one scene, his girlfriend, Chanice, who he has been stringing along for eight years, says, "Buck's a charming man who wants to remain a boy forever."

That is why Peter's first word to men is this: "Understand what a marriage ought to be, how each one is to function in their role, what is expected of you according to the Word of God."

Men must act with understanding and choose intelligently what comes into their homes. This is the number one responsibility of the husband in the home.

❖ What does it mean to understand your wife?

Your wife is not your cook, maid, or personal babysitter. She is your wife, an heir of this world, and a future ruler of the universe. One of the most important things you can work at is to understand her. You are to work with your wife in a way that honors her and honors God.

The first six verses of 1 Peter 3 are instructions for women. Why six verses? Because women were exploited in the ancient world (polygamy, rape, and divorce), Jesus lifted the status and position of women and marriage. Men are given only one verse, but it's powerful.

> You husbands, in the same way, live with your wives according to knowledge, giving honor to the woman, as to the more delicate vessel, as also being joint heirs of the grace of life, that your prayers may not be hindered. (1 Peter 3:7)

Living with your wife with understanding means, first of all, mutual submission. Prior to commanding wives to submit to their husbands, the apostle Paul taught that we are to submit to one another in the fear of God. Submission is the responsibility of husbands as well as of wives. A husband doesn't submit to his wife in his leadership capacity, but he must submit to the loving duty of being sensitive to the needs, fears, and feelings of his wife. In other words, a husband must subordinate his needs to hers, whether she is a Christian or not.

To live with your wife in an understanding way means to live with her "according to knowledge." Knowledge of what? Everything relevant: her, you, God, the Word, the situation, the kids—everything that's going on! This is generally a shock for most men.

Before marriage, young men are often incredibly independent. They go where they want, come in when they want, eat what they want, and wear what they want. Marriage means a second opinion is involved. Another set of desires, feelings, and ideas. Once again, playing a duet is much harder than playing a solo!

This calls for a lot of studying. Study her; study your responses to her. Nothing will reveal your sin and selfishness like your wife. Marriage is God's anvil for transformation to make us more like Christ. Marriage is wonderful if you can learn to live with constant conviction of selfishness and develop a willingness to change. Marriage reveals your self-deceptions. Marriage elicits responses of which we must repent that we would have never discovered on our own.

So I've got to learn about her. I've got to learn and reflect on myself. I also need the Word of God to instruct me so that I don't think in the selfish mold that the culture will try to press me into. This is a call to read, study, ponder, reflect, and ask lots of questions so that I can learn to live with her in an understanding way. Some important questions to ask are these:

- Will you help me understand?
- How do you feel about this?
- How are we doing?
- Can you tell me more?

Inform your leadership style with her perceptions. Take her into account before you make any important decisions. You may not appreciate her insight at the time, but it will likely be golden over the long term.

Understanding speaks of being sensitive to your wife's deepest physical and emotional needs. In other words, be thoughtful and respectful. You are to nourish and cherish her. Tragically, many women will say,

- My husband doesn't understand me.
- We never talk.
- He doesn't know how I feel or what I'm thinking about.
- I get the time he has left over.

Insensitivity builds walls in marriages. "Live with your wife in an understanding way" is another way of saying, "Be considerate." It isn't what you get out of marriage but what you put into it that brings glory to God.

Remember to date your wife. Use the date to let her know that you love being with her. Joy comes from being with someone who enjoys being with you. During your date, don't solve problems, don't dump on each other, and don't fix anything! Use conversation and active listening to explore the interior psychological map of one another.

Do you know and understand that your wife was designed to "long for you" (Genesis 3:16)?

She longs for your love, your protection, and your leadership. It is imperative to a woman that she feels secure in her husband's love, secure in the protection he can provide for her, both physical and emotional, and confidence in the wisdom of his leadership. Therefore, it is the husband's job to make her feel highly regarded, to honor her, to value her, and to protect her. As Paul says in Ephesians, it is to love her as his own body, to show honor to her under all conditions, to honor and love her *just as Christ loved the church* (Ephesians 5:25).

There will be times when your wife will not be easy to love, but an amazing man must determine to love her at all times. This, according to Peter, is man's second great responsibility in marriage. We must show courtesy and thoughtful consideration to our wives under every conceivable circumstance. One of the most devastating things that can occur in marriage is for the husband to become critical toward his wife, treating her with scorn or being sarcastic toward her. This is one of the major causes of unhappiness in marriage. This attitude threatens the basic nature of woman. It is the man's job to make his wife feel that she is important to him and to never take her for granted.

One of the most common complaints of wives to marriage counselors is the following:

> My husband just takes me for granted. To him, I'm just another appliance around the house. I'm only important to him for what I do for him, not for who I am.

This means that a wife is being threatened at the very deepest level of her being. She no longer feels secure in her husband's love and will likely react in a negative way.

❖ What does it mean to show honor to a more delicate vessel?

In the Olympics, men compete with women only in sailing, equestrian, and badminton events. That's it. Men are typically bigger, stronger, and faster. Billie Jean King beat Bobby Riggs, but that was a publicity stunt when she was twenty-nine and he was fifty-five. The difference is anatomical and biological. Men and women are equal, but they are not the same.

Women have strong feelings, strong minds, and strong wills.

They can, and often do, have stronger faith. An illustration of this is in terms of various kinds of household dishes. A man would be stoneware whereas a woman would be fine china. You can bang stoneware against the table, but you wouldn't think of doing it with china. It's more delicate, but also more expensive. Some believe that after God made Adam, he thought he could have done better.

The first six verses of 1 Peter 3 describe a woman who is fearless, with deep hope in God. She has a tranquility in her spirit that displays a high capacity of joy. Her behavior is pure and reverent, and her testimony is so profound that she can win over her husband with few or no words. Her inner self has the unfading beauty of a gentle and quiet spirit, which is of great worth in God's sight.

How do you honor her? You create a relationship and an environment that develops and appreciates her womanhood. When God established marriage, He knew that one of the greatest components for building worth into another person would be honor. That's why he tells husbands, "Give her honor as a fellow heir of the grace of life."

Webster defines honor as "high regard or great respect given; especially glory, fame; distinction."

Every marriage bond is susceptible to leakage. The world lures my wife with enticing, false promises of fulfillment and true significance. If I fail to honor her and esteem her as a woman of distinction, then I ignore the reality of her need and the deceptive power of the world's promises.

❖ What does it mean to be a fellow heir of the grace of life?

An amazing man understands the need for unlimited sharing of his own life with his wife in the most important part of his life: his spiritual life. She is a joint heir with you. What are you an heir of? Peter described our inheritance in 1 Peter 1:3–9.

- We are born into a new, eternal family.
- It's a living hope that cannot perish, spoil, or fade.
- It's kept in heaven and shielded by God's power.
- We can greatly rejoice, though now we may have to suffer a little.
- This endurance of our suffering will prove that our faith is genuine.
- Our faith is worth more than gold.
- This endurance will result in praise, glory, and honor when Jesus is revealed.
- We love and believe in a King we have never seen.
- We are filled with an inexpressible and glorious joy.
- The end result of our salvation is the salvation of our souls.

You are sleeping with a princess—a princess of the universe. Together you are learning to rule.

> Don't you know that the saints (the people of God) will judge the world? And if the world is judged by you, are you unworthy to judge the smallest matters? Don't you know that we will judge angels? How much more, things that pertain to this life? (1 Corinthians 6:2–3)

There's nothing more important to your family and to your wife than your spiritual leadership. Ephesians 6:4 teaches us that fathers are not to frustrate their children but to lead them and bring them up in the ways of the kingdom of God. A father, working in harmony with his wife, must be the leader in bringing up children in the training and instruction of the Lord.

❖ **What happens if I fail to practice these things?**

Failure by the husband to observe these things means spiritual poverty in the home. In fact, even your prayers would be hindered (1 Peter 3:7).

Prayer represents our whole spiritual relationship with God. If we cannot pray to God, our spiritual relationship to Him is in trouble. It is only God that can make human life worth living, and a man is a fool who tries to find a worthy life apart from God. That is the whole thrust of the gospel message. It is only in a restoration to God through Jesus Christ that men can find the intended worth and glory of a life well lived.

Swimming Upstream from the Culture

In our modern society—even in some churches—the different and complementary roles of biblical leadership for the husband and biblical pattern for a wife to entrust herself to her husband are despised or simply passed over. Some people just write them off as sub-Christian cultural leftovers from the first century.

But the first six verses of 1 Peter 3 describe a woman of stately stature. Peter's portrait of Christian womanhood is marked *first* by hope in God and *then* what grows out of that hope: fearlessness. She does not fear the future; she laughs at the future. The presence of hope in the invincible sovereignty of God drives out fear. Mature Christian women know that following Christ will mean suffering. But they believe the promises of God.

That is what godly women do: they entrust their souls to a faithful Creator. They hope in God. And they triumph over fear. They also *exert more effort and are more concerned with inner beauty than outer beauty.* They have the imperishable beauty of a gentle and quiet spirit. That spirit expresses itself in a unique trust with their husbands.

Four Kinds of Love

Love, as a word, describes an emotion with vastly differing degrees of intensity. We can say we love ice cream or chocolate, and we can pledge our love to a husband or wife until our dying breath.

Love is one of the most powerful emotions we can experience. Humans crave love from the moment of existence. And the Bible tells us that God *is* love. For Christian believers, love is the true test of genuine faith.

Four unique forms of love are found in the Bible. They are communicated through the following four Greek words:

- *eros*
- *storge*
- *philia*
- *agape*

Let's explore these different types of love characterized by romantic love, family love, brotherly love, and God's divine love. As we do, we'll discover what love really means and how to follow Jesus Christ's command to "love one another."

Eros is the Greek word for sensual or romantic love. The term originated from the mythological Greek goddess of love, sexual desire, physical attraction, and physical love. Even though the term is not found in the Old Testament, Song of Solomon vividly portrays the beauty and passion of erotic love.

Storge is a term for love in the Bible that you may not be familiar with. This Greek word describes family love, the affectionate bond that develops naturally between parents and children and between brothers and sisters. Many examples of family love are found in scripture, such as the mutual protection among Noah and his wife, the love of Jacob for his sons, and the strong love the sisters Martha and Mary had for their brother Lazarus.

Philia is the type of intimate love in the Bible that most Christians practice toward each other. This Greek term describes the powerful emotional bond seen in deep friendships. Philia is the most general type of love in scripture, encompassing love for fellow humans, care, respect, and compassion for people in need. The concept of brotherly love that unites believers is unique to Christianity.

Agape is the highest of the four types of love in the Bible. This term defines God's immeasurable, incomparable love for humankind. It is the divine love that comes from God. Agape love is perfect, unconditional, sacrificial, and pure. Jesus Christ demonstrated this kind of divine love to His Father and to all humanity in the way He lived and died.

How Linda and I Got Started

On a Saturday in the fall of 1969, at 7:30 p.m., a friend and I were waiting in the downstairs hall just outside of our church's youth room. We were home from college for the weekend and our youth leader had asked us to do a skit for the youth meeting. We had written a skit and only needed a girl to help us pull it off. The girl we had asked didn't show up so we had to go with plan B. At 7:35 p.m., Linda came walking down the hall. I said, "Linda, can you help us out with a skit?" She said, "Do I have to say anything?" I said, "No, just sashay in with a piece of paper." "I can do that," she said. That was it. That was the beginning. The next time I was home from college, I asked her on a date. She first said yes, but then almost called it off. Her mother had to encourage her to go with me, and we've been together ever since. On a hot August 12, 1972, she took my hand and said, "I do!" We still do skits, only now it's called life. I think 'em up, she sashays, and we entertain each other. It's never boring, and she still thinks I'm magnetic.

Marriage: A Picture of the Trinity and Christ

A man and a woman are commanded to *be glued to* one another in marriage. All of life's adventures, joys, and trials are to be experienced together. Couples are reminded that to do this, they must leave their past behind and rely mentally, emotionally, physically, and spiritually on one another.

Though the Son is God and equal to the Father, He entrusts Himself to the will of the Father. It is the woman who, by faith, demonstrates the unique oneness of God. She, like Jesus Christ, entrusts herself to her husband. When she does, she initiates unity. This oneness is the most beautiful picture of God's image that we'll see on earth.

Just as a marriage is a model of the oneness of God, it is also a picture of the love of God. Husbands are to love their wives just as Christ loved the church and gave his life for her. (Ephesians 5:25)

This is the command of scripture. It is the man who demonstrates the love of God. A man's love for his wife should be such that he would willingly lay down his life for her. When a man is willing to lay down his life for his bride, it is easy for her to entrust herself to him. He is magnetic.

Questions for Chapter 16

1. Scripture tells a husband to live with his wife "in an understanding way" and to love his wife "just as Christ loved the church." On a 1 to 10 scale, how well would you rate yourself in doing these things? How would your wife rate you?
2. Of the eleven quick guidelines listed at the beginning of this chapter, which are your top three strengths and which are your lowest three weaknesses? Which will you want to focus on to improve, starting today?
3. How can you avoid being a "boy forever" and take your responsibility more seriously to be a leader in your home?
4. How might you be able to understand your wife more completely?
5. What does it mean to you "to show honor to your wife, especially in light of the fact that she is a fellow heir of the grace of life"? In what ways might you need to improve in showing honor to her?
6. As you attempt to love one another, especially your wife, how can you do so better by understanding the four types of love described as romantic love, family love, brotherly love, and God's divine love?
7. Do you strive to be the kind of amazing husband who treats his wife with the realization that others will see it as a picture of the Trinity and Christ? What would it mean for you and your wife if you did this more consistently?

Chapter 17

"BE INSPIRATIONAL": INVESTING YOUR LIFE

How Does a Man Invest His Life?

To inspire someone is to breathe life into them.

Inspiration is one of the greatest gifts you can give to anyone, especially to young people. When you inspire others, it gives them life. Inspiration multiplies, making ripples over time like a pebble thrown into a lake. It is powerful. Inspiring one other person can eventually touch dozens of lives, perhaps hundreds, thousands, or more. The power of inspiration is unlimited.

Fathers and Elders

How to Mentor as a Father

The mentoring journey begins when you become the father of a four-year-old. Being a father (or a surrogate father) typically brings out the best in a man, and you can't be amazing without fulfilling that role. As your children grow, you will grow with them—sometimes just slightly ahead of them.

I was twenty-one when I married Linda, and twenty-two when our first daughter, Jacqui, was born. As she got a bit older, I remember going into her room every morning and she would be standing up, holding the rails on her crib—red hair, big ol' eyes, and a wide smile. We'd bring her back to our bed, talk and laugh, and eventually all go back to sleep. We continued that routine with the next three kids, and the laughter, as well the noise level, increased.

We ate our meals together, especially supper. Everyone had their own spot at the table. Jacqui and I usually started the conversation, but everyone joined in—more laughter. It was a sacred hour and phone calls were not allowed. Eventually their friends caught on and the only voices to be heard between 5 and 6 p.m. were familiar family voices.

We encouraged them to try different things—baseball, softball, tennis, piano, ballet, track, and school band. I taught them all how to ride a bike and to throw a ball. I coached them, and Linda was their biggest cheerleader. We also read the Bible and prayed together.

Their teenage years were more challenging, especially for one of our daughters. It was a painful time, but our family never gave up on each other. I believe a key difference between a good family and a bad family is that bad families give up on each other and good families don't.

All of our children are adults now, and we are proud of each one. Now we even have teenage grandchildren.

I mentor my children as adults only when they ask for it. I have opportunities at times to teach my grandchildren how to ski and golf. We also talk and text by phone. We get together for meals and holidays and there are storytelling and—you guessed it—laughter. I have grown and they have grown, and we've been on the journey together. We could not have made it without certain practices. What should you practice as a parent?

Be generous with love and encouragement.

> Being affectionately desirous of you, we were ready to share with you not only the gospel of God but also our own selves, because you had become very dear to us. (1 Thessalonians 2:8)

Communicate with your children. Tell them, "I love you, I'm proud of you, and this is what you're good at."

Be sure your love is unconditional.

Express it through frequent verbal and physical reminders. Praise them for the special way that God has made them, privately and in public. This creates a love bond with them.

Express your love by constantly praying for them. You are in partnership with God so don't rely on your own strength. Depend on God to work in their lives. Pray daily and specifically for each one of your children and their various needs.

Be available. Let them know that they are your priority. Build their needs into your schedule. Enjoy being with them when they're angry, fearful, sad, disgusting, filled with shame, or overcome with despair. Your joy will help them return to joy as you sync up with them when life is challenging. Help them to know they can always run to your open arms. Teach them that they can do the same with their Heavenly Father.

Encourage them, affirm them, and motivate them to do their best. When they lose or fail, teach them to be gracious. Teach them that they can't be anything they want to be, but they can be all that God has meant for them to be. Encourage them with a vision of what God could do with their lives if they were wholly yielded to him. Teach them to exercise faith in every situation.

Lead an authentic life.

> You are my witnesses, and God also, how holy and righteous and blameless was our conduct toward you. (1 Thessalonians 2:10)

Give them a Christlike example to follow. Admit your failures and weaknesses as a father and, when necessary, humble yourself and seek forgiveness. Over time, they will discover these things anyhow. You don't have to be perfect.

Love your wife, their mother. They'll get more security from that than anything else. You are partners in the parenting enterprise. You each bring something that your children need. Share common commitments, goals, friends, burdens, values, priorities, and ministry.

Make sure they see you reading and studying God's Word and praying. One day, my son, Josh, walked into my bedroom without knocking. I was on the side of the bed praying. He said, "Oh, sorry, Dad." I was glad he walked in to see me praying.

Talk to them about the scripture and how it's impacting you. You don't have to be a scholar, but you should be interacting with it at least four days a week.

Teach them to stand for what they believe even if it's not what everyone else is doing. Protect them from the corruption of this world. Teach them about the spiritual battle they are engaged in and how to wage spiritual warfare. Show them how to respond to adversity with calm confidence in the sovereignty of God and gratitude for the goodness of God, especially in times of prosperity and abundance.

Give them godly leadership and exhortation.

Instruction in the ways of God is meant to be a vital part of the culture of our family life. Everyday occurrences should be responded to and evaluated from a biblical perspective. "Family devotions" are really meant to be an around-the-clock way of living (1 Thessalonians 2:11).

Instruction includes reproof and correction. And it's not just about unacceptable behavior. It's about attitudes, responses, and values. Be fair and consistent in your discipline.

Help them develop heroes with character. Tell them or encourage them to read/watch stories of true greatness.

Give them a godly vision for their lives and futures. Brainstorm with them about their potential and their plans. Impress on their hearts that God wants to use them, that their lives could be extraordinary, for His glory.

Finally, leave a godly legacy. Leaving a godly legacy for your children should be the goal of all amazing fathers. Although the faith and godliness of your children is ultimately the work of the Holy Spirit, God uses the influence of fathers and mothers to make a great impact on their children.

> The apostle John says that his greatest joy is to have his children walking in the faith. (3 John 4)

How to Mentor as an Elder

I have had the privilege of mentoring not only my own children but also a number of men over the last fifty years. I started as a coach fresh out of college. I gave them baseball, basketball, and life skills instruction. When I went into the ministry, I continued coaching and mentoring. I helped young men grow strong in their faith and put together road maps for their lives. Now I'm an elder. My motto is "I'll meet you anytime, anywhere, anyplace to talk about anything you want to." That is the work of an elder.

The original mentor is a character in Homer's epic poem *The Odyssey*. When Odysseus, king of Ithaca, went to fight in the Trojan War, he entrusted the care of his kingdom to Mentor. Mentor served as the teacher and overseer of Odysseus's son, Telemachus.

The dictionary defines a mentor as "a trusted counselor or guide." Others expand on that definition by suggesting that a mentor is "someone who is helping you with your career, specific work projects, or general life advice out of the goodness of his or her heart."

A mentor is a personal advocate, not so much in the public setting but in life. A trusted mentor can help with personal and professional growth. They challenge young people to think differently and to open their eyes and their mind to other ideas and opportunities. Everyone can benefit by having a good mentor.

What a Mentor Does

A mentor

- takes a long-range view on growth and development
- helps mentees see the destination but doesn't always give the detailed map to get there
- offers encouragement and cheerleading

The key verse for mentoring is

> Counsel in the heart of man is like deep water, but a man of understanding will draw it out. (Proverbs 20:5)

Wisdom lies *deep* within a man or woman, like a hidden reservoir ready in the season of need. The metaphor is of a well whose waters are far beneath the surface of the ground so that one must use a bucket with a long rope to draw water to the surface. Thus, a person's dreams and motives are deep in that they are difficult to extract. You should know how to not only get wisdom but to use it. The wise man—the *man of understanding*—knows how to draw wisdom *out* for practical and ready use. This is often done with powerful questions, such as the following:

- Where would you like to be in one year, two years, or five years?
- Where are you right now?
- What is your next step to move you where you'd like to be?
- What are the next three steps?
- What's working in your life?
- What's not working?
- What do you need to change?

There are four sequential steps to help someone develop a skill.

1. I do; you watch.
2. I do; you help.
3. You do; I help.
4. You do; I watch.

There are seven practical life skills for mentees.

1. Show up on time.
2. Do the homework.
3. Remember people's names.
4. Be OK with *not* being great at everything.
5. Follow through quickly.
6. Take your work seriously.
7. Be able to laugh at yourself.

Mentoring in the Scriptures

Moses and Jethro

One of the first instances of mentoring in the Old Testament is the example of Jethro and Moses. Here are some things observations about mentoring from their relationship in Exodus 18.

First, the foundation of mentoring is a close relationship (Exodus 18:1–8).

In these verses, we see the closeness of these men. They greeted one another. They were concerned about each other's welfare. They spent time together talking. They told each other about what was going on in their lives. Their relationship had been cultivated over the forty-year period that Moses was a shepherd in the wilderness (Exodus 3:1).

Sometimes we focus too much on the training and not enough on the relationship. Without a close relationship built by trust, love, and mutual commitment, effective mentoring will be unlikely.

Second, the only way a mentoring relationship will work is if there is transparency (Exodus 18:8).

Moses was willing to tell what was going on. Moses told Jethro everything that had happened to him (Exodus 18:8).

Moses was willing to be vulnerable. He was willing to admit fears, weaknesses, mistakes, and concerns. Jethro was as transparent as Moses.

Third, the mentor must genuinely desire the best for his protégé (Exodus 18:9–12).

Jethro was very excited about how God had blessed and used Moses. Moses's victory was Jethro's victory. He was happy when things were going well for Moses. He got at least as excited as, if not more excited than, Moses over what God had done for him. He threw a big feast for Moses, Aaron, and all the elders of Israel. We should celebrate the successes of those we are mentoring. We should be their biggest cheerleaders. Rather than speaking of our own accomplishments, we should be listening actively to how God is working in their lives.

Fourth, mentors make positive investments in the lives of those they are mentoring (Exodus 18:13–23).

Moses's leadership was incomplete. He was a new leader. He led Israel well in times of crisis, but he was not so good at overseeing the day-to-day affairs of the people. Moses had to learn that different seasons of leadership require different leadership skills. A mentor is there to help continue developing those he is training.

Moses tried to do everything himself (Exodus 18:13).

He did all the judging. We are not sure why he took on so much. Maybe it was a lack of trust, ignorance, or overestimating his own ability. Whatever the reason, he thought he was doing right. Ironically, he was not training and mentoring others.

Jethro helped Moses develop as a leader and trainer of others. He questioned Moses's method. He then pointed out why his method was not good: it was not good for Moses because he was going to wear down, and it was not good for the people because they had to wait all day. It was not good for the work of God because his trying to do everything was actually hindering the effectiveness of God's people.

Jethro offered wise counsel. He didn't tell Moses to stop judging or being a representative of the people to God. He didn't tell him to stop teaching God's laws and how to live. He came up with a very helpful suggestion. He told him to choose out of the people able men of character who could help and to let these men do some of the judging. As a result of Jethro's counsel, things were easier for Moses and the people were better served.

Fifth, mentoring is only possible with teachable people (Exodus 18:24–26).

There were many reasons that Moses might not have listened.

- He had already been greatly used by God.
- He was already leading a huge number of people.
- He could have thought, *You are just my father-in-law. What do you know?*
- He could have feared letting others get involved and losing control.

Moses was known for his meekness and humility (Numbers 2:3).

Moses followed Jethro's suggestion. He chose able men out of Israel and set up leaders over the people. Mentoring only works with teachable people.

Moses was mentored by Jethro and he, in turn, mentored Joshua. Both of them were amazing men. Joshua went on to lead the nation into the Promised Land. As noted at the beginning of this chapter, mentoring can have a powerful impact.

The Apostle Paul: Father and Elder

As we said earlier, the apostle Paul didn't just lead people to Christ. He built a spiritual family. He was a father with many sons.

He built relationships with these sons and mentored them as their spiritual father. Paul sent Timothy to the Corinthians as a model of maturity to emulate. He would help them build a multigenerational community in which weak and strong lived together (1 Corinthians 4:15–17).

The world today is in dire need of fathers and elders—men with life experience who walk with God. This is how an amazing man closes the loop and finishes well. Go and be that man!

Questions for Chapter 17

1. In the section "How to Mentor as a Father," there are a lot of suggestions on how to do this effectively. Which of these prompted you to think that you could do better? What next steps could you take to become more amazing as a mentor?
2. As you read through the section "What a Mentor Does," what stood out for you? What will you start, stop, continue, or improve in your role as a mentor?
3. What did you learn from the biblical examples of fathers and elders?
4. Do you perceive the grandfather/elder stage to be as important as it is presented in this chapter? If so, and you are at this stage in your life, how can you become amazing at this role, which is so needed by young people these days?

Now
it's up to you!

Amazing Men Ministries is available to help you on your
journey toward amazingness. See amazingmenminstries.com.

Printed in the United States
by Baker & Taylor Publisher Services